Empowered!

Fight for What Matters.
Build What Lasts.

Ginger Gann, Sarah Neal, Amy Spear, and Carol Sasnett

Worthy Pursuit Ministries

WESTBOW
PRESS®
A DIVISION OF THOMAS NELSON
& ZONDERVAN

rin – dad

nn fr Parker – dad

WestBow Press books may be ordered through booksellers or by contacting:

WestBow Press
A Division of Thomas Nelson & Zondervan
1663 Liberty Drive
Bloomington, IN 47403
www.westbowpress.com
1 (866) 928-1240

ISBN: 978-1-9736-9300-0 (sc)
ISBN: 978-1-9736-9301-7 (hc)
ISBN: 978-1-9736-9299-7 (e)

Library of Congress Control Number: 2020909745

Print information available on the last page.

WestBow Press rev. date: 7/7/2020

Empowered: Fight for What Matters—Build What Lasts is a four-week journal meant to be used alongside your Bible, during quiet moments of daily prayer and meditation. Through a short devotional message, you will be encouraged and inspired to live life empowered, beyond your everyday chaos.

Each day includes a Bible passage followed by a personal story and short devotional. The "Fight" section, at the end of each day, will lead you into a time of self-reflection with a goal of awakening the inner warrior within you. The "Build" section will provide tools for seeking godly wisdom, power, and provision for living life fully empowered.

Contents

Acknowledgments

This book is dedicated to all the precious women who have allowed us to minister in their churches. It is one of the biggest privileges we could be asked to do! God has blessed us with knowing each of you, and we look forward to the next time.

We want to thank our families, who have allowed us to spend time away to write, study, travel, teach, and plan. None of this would have been possible without your encouragement and all the times you had to perform double duty while we were away. We love you all so much and pray God's blessings for you always!

Sincerely,
Ginger Gann
Sarah Neal
Carol Sasnett
Amy Spear

Introduction

Tucked between the pages of the Old Testament is an old story of great value for us, even today. Nehemiah's story, though ancient, is still alive and carries the potential to change the legacy of our generation for the glory of God.

Driven by overwhelming compassion for the people of Israel, a man's life is suddenly interrupted to pursue a higher calling. This God-initiated burden of the heart compelled Nehemiah to pick up his sword and fight for what mattered most.

Through Nehemiah's life, we discover God has a divine appointment scheduled for each of us. His invitation compels us with compassion and prompts us toward our personal commission. But rest assured, God not only commissions us to go beyond doing good and loving others but also equips us for the task.

Grab your hammer and pick up your sword, mighty warrior, because you are not only appointed—you are empowered to

- pursue your passion and purpose beyond the chaos,
- live authentically side by side,
- fight your way forward to victory in spite of opposition, and
- leave a legacy for God's glory!

We are delighted to take this journey with you, to lock arms, forming an army to build what stands the test of time and fight for what matters most!

> Don't be afraid of them. Remember the Lord, who is great and awesome, and fight for your families, your sons and your daughters, your wives and your homes. (Nehemiah 4:14 NIV)

Week One

Following Your Commission

Day One

Tissue, Please!

Today's scripture reading: John 16:33; Philippians 4:6–7

"Do people of *real* faith worry? If so, what can be done about it?"

I really want to know the answer to these questions. Although I consider myself a woman of faith, I worry. I'll blame it all on my genes; it runs in my family. Like my mother before me, I will go as far to say to my children, "It's my *job* to worry. I'm the mom, and it's what I do." I'm a generational worrier. Worse yet, we are also criers one and all, even the men. We are passionate and demonstratively expressive criers, meaning we don't cry silently! When we get a heart full of something, we want others to know about it. The truth is my heart is full. I'm deeply troubled about many things happening in our world today, and I want you to know about it.

I wish we could sit over coffee together. I would love to hear what fills your heart. I would guess you are deeply troubled too. I wonder whether any items on your worry list match mine. What you worry about is important to me. Truly, it is. What you do with your worries has an impact on my life, on yours, and on the lives of our families. It's our collective decisions about the issues of the heart that determine what comes in and goes out of our communal gates. Together, we stand watch! With each decision, we either chip away at the crumbling wall of morality or build it up. Our collective choices, yours and mine, determine the rubble that will be left behind for our children to sort through. We monitor the ebb and flow of social norms and establish our mutual accountability.

So I admit it: all things considered, I tend to worry. When I see how we treat one another, I want to cry. When I see the collateral damage from our day-to-day choices, my heart breaks. Even though my head knows what the Bible verses for the day reveal, my heart wants to keep worrying in all the places where God's Word tells me I should be trusting. Because let's face it: —it's a rough world out here.

For the sake of time, let me get to my point. While studying the life of Nehemiah, God began to teach me the difference between a heart full of compassion and a heart filled with plain old worry. Now, I'd like to share what I've learned with you.

Disclaimer: My friend, if after our time together, you too come out on the other side of these pages a crier like me, it's okay! A soft, compassionate heart is not only a good thing; I believe it's a God thing! Why? Because Nehemiah's life journal teaches that it's the God-initiated compassion within that propels us forward, catapulting us into the center of His divine purpose.

I'm so thankful you're joining the conversation this week, where we are encouraged to

- go beyond worry to compassion,
- go beyond compassion to commission, and
- go beyond commission to step boldly into God's appointed purpose—completely equipped and fully empowered!

Grab your coffee (or other drink), and let's talk about how we can go from worrier to warrior! Amen? Amen!

Heavenly Father, thank You in advance for revealing Yourself to me as I spend time with You through Your Word and this material. I pray I am encouraged, enlightened, equipped, and fully empowered to live forward—fearlessly in Your will. I want to faithfully fight for what is right (in Your sight) and build what lasts (for Your glory).

In Jesus's name, amen.

Reflect and Respond

The Bible says God is:

- The one and only God (James 2:19)
- The God of angel armies/the Lord Almighty (Psalm 46)
- The one for whom nothing is too hard (Jeremiah 32:27; Matthew 19:26)
- Abba Father (Romans 8:15)
- Love (1 John 4:16)
- Faithful (Hebrews 10:23)
- Peace (Philippians 4:7)

Please note that this is by no means an exhaustive list. Our God is mighty, and His character is found on every page of the scriptures.

Fight

Whom do *you* believe God is? Where does this personal view of God have its foundation? Here are some examples.

- I believe God is ever present—from my personal experience.
- I believe God is the God of Christmas and Easter; it's what I was taught/raised to believe.
- I believe God is uninvolved—comparing what I've read He has done for others and what He has done or not done for me.
- I believe God is _____ from/because of _____.
- Spend a few moments journaling and meditating on where your value of God has its foundation. Who do you say God is, and why? peace, love, sovereign, on this earth thru his spirit, works this eg. works all thing for good. we just can't always see til later -apple pie -apple cider vinegar

Build

Spend time in prayer. Ask God to help you align your understanding of who He is with His truth.

Day Two

Red Roasters, Roosters, and Fingernails

Today's scripture reading: James 1:5; 2 Timothy 3:16–17

Each year, my husband and I travel with my cousin and her husband to Gatlinburg, Tennessee. On one particular trip, Teresa and I visited a cast iron shop in search of a roasting pan my head was set on purchasing. I spotted six quarts of perfect cast iron sitting on the second shelf of aisle three, but a quick peek at the price tag told me to keep shopping. However, as I was turning to go, I noticed four shelves above the roasting pan sat a beautiful, bright red ceramic rooster. Be still, my heart! I asked the lady wearing the name tag and cute little apron the price. She grabbed a stepladder and climbed up to deliver the news: $130. Sulking with my head down and bottom lip forward, I found Teresa near the silicone cooking mitts with the red and green chili peppers on them.

While I told her my tale, she interrupted me. "How many times do you ever buy anything for yourself? You need to go on and get that rooster." She was right! I rarely buy myself anything. After numerous failed attempts at calling my husband at the knife store across the street, I sent a text in hopes of infiltrating the metal barrier. Then I met up with Teresa near the cash registers. The lady in the cute apron asked if we were ready to check out.

I explain to her my dilemma—how I really want the red rooster but can't ask my husband due to no cell phone reception. The cute apron lady looked up at me from under her big hair, smiled, and bent her apple-red index finger to motion me closer. Then with an accent as thick as her lipstick, she said, "Well, hun, just don't ask him then."

I scraped skin off two knuckles going after my wallet before I heard the beep of my phone. Teresa leaned in over my shoulder, and we slowly peered down to read the text from my husband, which said, "Just get whatever you want." Happy dance! Wrapped up like a mummy in butcher paper and tucked inside double bags, the rooster left the store with me.

Upon leaving the cabin that morning, my head had been fully committed to purchasing a roasting pan, but my heart sold me out to an overpriced ceramic rooster. When this rooster seized my attention, a battle immediately broke out between logic and emotion. "I don't need a $130 ceramic rooster, and I sure can't afford it," said Logic. "But it is so stinkin' cute, and I do have a credit card," replied Emotion. In the scope of things, spending $130 isn't world changing, especially because checking with my hubby confirmed I wasn't spending our gas money for the trip back home. However, the experience got me thinking about the method I use for making decisions in my life, big and small.

I'm a grown woman, so I don't *need* endorsement from my husband. I'm a human being created with free will, so I don't *have* to ask approval from my God. Nevertheless, I lovingly respect and honor them both; their perspective is precious to me. Seeking wisdom from God and good counsel from my life partner is not an obligation—it is a benefit, a blessing, and my joy. They serve as my compass, inspiration, and confirmation.

Reflect and Respond

In the ongoing battle between your head and your heart, how do you decide on a winner? Who or what wins your attention, time, resources, energy, or emotions?

Fight

List three of your greatest influences when making important decisions.

God -usually only big things

Corbe -

mom

Build

Beginning today, will you consider adding at least one of the tools below to your list of influencers?

- Daily prayer for wisdom for your decisions ahead
- Memorize James 1:5
- Filter decisions through the life examples of those found in your daily reading of the scriptures
- Memorize 2 Timothy 3:16

James 1:5 If any of you lacks wisdom, he should ask God, who gives generously to all without finding fault, and it will be given to Him.

Tim 3:14 All scripture is God-breathed and is useful for teaching, rebuking, correcting and training in righteousness

Day Three

Confessions of a Worrier

Today's scripture reading: Nehemiah 1:4

Although most folks probably wouldn't say they enjoy spending time in the Old Testament, I want to ask you to sit with me for a few minutes to do just that. There is someone I'd like us to visit: Nehemiah.

Nehemiah is an Israelite whose story is mainly told in the Old Testament book of Nehemiah. He worked for King Artaxerxes.[1] The primary obligation of his position was to keep the king alive by tasting his food and drink before he ate (in case someone disagreed with the king's politics and tried to poison him). But with good security in place, it was also a prestigious job. A cupbearer was someone whom the king knew and trusted. Nehemiah lived a very fine and comfortable life. If left to his own self-guidance, Nehemiah was content to live out the rest of his days right there in good ol' Susa.

However, the Bible tells us in Proverbs 16:9 (NIV), "In their heart humans plan their course, but the LORD directs his steps." Exactly. We will see that God is about to interrupt Nehemiah's well-packaged life and redirect his steps all the way to Jerusalem.

Meeting up with Nehemiah today, we find the Israelites were no longer held in captivity by King Nebuchadnezzar, the former ruler of Babylon. For some time now, little by little, the Jews were returning home. However, there was no welcome wagon waiting to greet them. Instead, they arrived to find the wall, previously surrounding this once great city,

---

[1] Herbert Edward Ryle, "Nehemiah 1," *Cambridge Bible for Schools and Colleges* (1901). Bible Hub, http://biblehub.com/commentaries/cambridge/nehemiah/1.htm.

in ruin. With no wall or gate to monitor the ebb and flow of the city, and without administrators sitting at these gates to oversee civil law and order, Jerusalem was merely a campground—and a dangerous one at that. After seventy years of captivity in Babylon, the Israelites returned to find the holy temple exposed and their homeland, heritage, and future still threatened by a relentless enemy.

One day, Nehemiah's brother and a few other men paid him a nine-hundred-mile visit from Jerusalem in order to give Nehemiah an update on how things were going for the people back home. It was not good news. In Nehemiah 1:3 (NIV), we read, "They said to me, 'Those who survived the exile and are back in the province are in great trouble and disgrace. The wall of Jerusalem is broken down, and its gates have been burned with fire." His brother gravely described a Jerusalem that in no way resembled the glorious city of their forefathers.

Nehemiah's heart broke as he listened. Nehemiah 1:4 (NIV) says, "When I heard these things, I sat down and wept. For some days I mourned and fasted and prayed before the God of heaven." He was broken for his people, his friends, his family, and the once great nation of Israel, which would be completely lost if something was not done. Nehemiah was overwhelmed by the thought of it all. I think it's safe to say God had Nehemiah's full attention. It looks like we may have something in common with our new friend Nehemiah: he may be a bit of a worrier too.

Reflect and Respond

Sometimes when trouble calls, the walls of our faith may crack or even crumble. When our hearts and minds are left exposed, without the protective wall of God's blessed assurance, doubt and worry will easily overtake us.

Fight

Spend a few moments surveying the walls of your confidence in God. Is there an area of your life where your faith in God is cracked or crumbling? Is there an area of your life where worry has conquered your confidence? *- not a big worrier - small things Sometimes w/ Sutton*

Build

- sometime I wonder if my lack of worry is from ignoring things - not going to God enough

Like Nehemiah in chapter 1 and particularly verse 4, go before the God of heaven in prayer and ask Him

- to be attentive to the concerns of your heart,
- to stand watch over your thoughts and emotions to defeat any doubt, and
- to rebuild your assurance in Him alone.

Day Four

Live and Let Live

Advocating for a world where everything is acceptable will put you in a group with the open-minded. Unrestricted living sounds very contemporary, doesn't it? It's very progressive. Very Hollywood! Life without limits is increasingly becoming the new norm. Yet life without good boundaries is not an ideal concept —our planet is much too small. Our actions, behaviors, and choices rub up against each other too closely. Everything is not okay.

It is no exaggeration to say self-indulgence and instant gratification run rampant in today's culture. This current mind-set to live and let live gives permission to seek after the cravings of the heart with no thought of consequence beyond satisfying momentary desires. However, it's not hard to spot the negative effect this approach has on us. In reality, when this methodology is set into motion outside the plumb line of moral standards, we are exposed to all varieties of chaos. We see the impact infiltrating our homes, schools, churches, and communities.

We shouldn't be surprised. Scripture warns us in James 1:15 (NIV), "Then, after desire has conceived it gives birth to sin; and sin, when it is full-grown, gives birth to death." Have you noticed evil isn't even trying to hide? It lives right out in the daylight with a big smile on its face, proud, flourishing, and carrying signs. I can't watch the news. I can barely tolerate Facebook. We simply agree to disagree —you live your life your way, and I'll live my life my way. While trying hard to not be labeled narrow-minded or not appear judgmental, little is done to prevent the consequential impact of the choices we make from spreading like a cancer. Sadly, well-meaning folks perpetuate the outcome with their silence. It's a difficult situation we find ourselves in, when we survey the state of our common society. People everywhere are dying physically, spiritually, mentally, and emotionally? I wonder (yes, and I worry) about these things.

It may sound odd, but I also give God glory and praise about these things. No, not for the sin and pain rampaging society, but because it is through my personal heartache over such where God grabs my attention. It's smack-dab in the middle of this heartache where He interrupts my pretty little world, for crying out loud. Fortunately, God uses His relentless compassion (aka our worry and fear that we can't shake off) for His intentional purpose. If we're listening, He completely turns around our selfie-obsessed hearts. He rotates our lenses outward, using our sympathy and empathy to thrust each of us into the center of His divine purpose and into our God-assigned commission of compassion. God is surveying the damage, and what He sees breaks His heart too. Something must be done. So I ask you, who is going to do the work of demonstrating compassion by sharing Jesus's love if not you and I? My heart breaks, and yours should too.

When God sent Nehemiah's brother with news of Jerusalem's plight, He grabbed more than just Nehemiah's attention; He also grabbed his heart. For four solid months, Nehemiah fasted and prayed, but his prayer meetings were more than a pity party for a few old friends. His compassion was more than just a "bless their heart" compulsion, more than worry. He couldn't let go. Something must be done! Nehemiah didn't know what or how, but he was beginning to see who.

Reflect and Respond

Saying yes when God compels us to action enables us, through Him, to sow a little grace and good into the chaos around us. Even though individually we may not be able to control, stop, or affect change to the overall big picture, we can individually make a difference wherever He compels, commissions, appoints, equips, and empowers us. Each one of us can be the answer on the other side of individual prayer, but we must invite God to interrupt our days and grab our attention. We must be determined to say yes and then act accordingly on His behalf to fight for what's right and build what will last.

Fight

Make a list of what is grabbing your attention and your compassion. What breaks your heart?

Sexuality & gender crisis

Build

Take your list and talk it over with the Lord. Go beyond worry. Write down any thoughts that come to mind about how you can individually make a difference where He is compelling you.

Day Five

Well, Bless Your Heart!

Today's scripture reading: Philemon 1:7

After buying the rooster, Teresa and I left the cast iron shop and walked across the street to reunite with Jimmy and Larry at the knife store. I felt pretty content with my rooster resting on my lap as our pickup truck pulled out of the parking lot. When we arrived back at our cabin, I placed my rooster into the capable hands of my husband while reminding him to be very careful. Somehow, though, in the short distance between the truck and the front door, my husband thought the bag was easier to carry while supporting it from the bottom and, acting on this thought, turned the rooster sideways. This was when we hear the crash.

The four of us stood in the driveway like a bunch of deer in headlights, looking down at the bag lying on the blacktop. Then, as if someone pressed fast-forward, Teresa and Larry shot off for the cabin faster than I had ever seen either one of them move before.

"I told you to be careful! I told you it would break! I told you it was ceramic!" I managed to say through my disbelief.
"Ceramic! Well, who makes a roasting pan out of ceramic?"
"Roasting pan? It's not a roaster—it's a rooster!"
"A rooster? A *rooster*? You paid $130 for a rooster?"
"Well, you said to get whatever I want!"

I ran straight into the bedroom and put myself in time out because I needed a minute. I could hear the mumbling coming from the front room and decided there was nothing to be done now but to go survey the damage. An awkward silence fell over the cabin as I entered the room. While attempting to peel open the butcher paper, I could hear the pieces rattle and stopped; it was just too painful. Disheartened, I looked up across the room at my husband with tears in my eyes.

Right then, in an attempt to rescue his best friend and salvage the rest of our vacation time together, Larry came straight over and gave me a big bear hug. "You know he feels awful, don't ya? You know he didn't mean to, don't ya?"

"But I loved that rooster."

"I know you did," Larry said while patting me on the back. "Bless your heart!"

He spoke words of truth about my husband to my heart, all the while encouraging me and not discounting how I felt.

In hindsight, I clearly see even though Larry couldn't salvage my rooster, he did save the day. He acted on his compassion by offering a bit of comfort to both me and my husband. He hadn't personally experienced love for a piece of ceramic, yet out of love for me, as a friend, he offered some good, old-fashioned sympathy. However, his compassion compelled him to action with empathy on behalf of his buddy Jimmy. It came from personally knowing the pain and remorse felt as a result of an unhappy wife. Through this simple display of sympathy and empathy, Jimmy and I received a gentle reminder of the unmatched value in the gift of grace and forgiveness.

This story, though sad, is only about a piece of ceramic. However, on any given day, there is a God-appointed assignment ready and waiting for each of us; a divine appointment with our name on it, to offer the same. At just the right time, our God will come calling with His relentless compassion to commission you as His agent. The assignment may be a big job or one as small as a smile, but we are each commissioned to serve on His behalf to offer encouragement and grace for the greater good and for His glory!

When we are willing, a relentless compassion can take us beyond a "Bless your heart" sympathy all the way to God-inspired empathy that acts, moves, and does.

But don't be anxious! What God appoints, He will equip. What He equips, He will empower. God will empower you to boldly pick up your hammer and your sword, to fight for what matters most, and to build what lasts in your heart, in your home, in your community, and in your world.

Reflect and Respond

Your God-given appointment is waiting. It may be the thing He is repeatedly bringing to your attention, this thing He wants you through sympathy to offer others as a gift of grace, encouragement, forgiveness, hope, or love. On the other hand, your appointment could involve the very thing you're in the middle of right now, something you can't even talk about yet because it's too raw and too painful. Your empathetic heart already knows that by His grace and through His power, when you come through to the other side of this thing, you're going right back in for other survivors. Where is God's compassion taking you today?

Fight

Pray to the God of heaven and ask Him to fully equip you with all you need, enabling you to recognize His presence in every situation where He compels you through His compassion and prompts you toward your personal commission.

Build

Write down any thoughts that come to mind about your experiences with both sympathy and empathy.

Now, consider where you can take action to demonstrate sympathy and empathy toward someone God has brought into your life.

Day Six

From Compassion to Purpose

What is your favorite comfort food? With what memory is it seasoned?

Every memory I have as a child, while recovering from any illness, is attached to my mom's homemade potato soup. Each family gathering holds visions of picnics and BBQ grills. Every birthday, there was crisp, fried salmon patties (if you're not from the South, just google it). Sweet memories of my mother's favorite recipes and family reunions not only make my mouth water, they make my heart happy too. Food is nutritious, yes, but it is also soothing, satisfying, and comforting.

Even so, the Bible tells us our friend Nehemiah went without food for four solid months. Not one bite of chocolate! Why in the world would anyone volunteer to *not* eat? I suppose sometimes life circumstances happen in ways where even potato soup won't bring comfort.

When God sent Nehemiah's brother to Susa with news of Jerusalem's plight, He grabbed more than just Nehemiah's attention—He also grabbed his heart. Nehemiah set a goal to obtain clear discernment about what role he should play in God's sovereign purpose regarding the Israelite people. In days of old, food is shared from preparation time through consumption. Mealtime is an extended time of socialization; Nehemiah's decision to abstain from eating was a choice to remove all distraction while seeking God's full purpose. It was a time of self-preparation because saying yes to becoming God's man for the job would be life-altering. Nehemiah would leave behind the comfort and security of his current position and status. His only certainty was knowing he would face constant uncertainty in the days ahead.

When I heard these words, I sat down and wept. I mourned for a number of days, fasting and praying before the God of heaven ... let Your eyes be open and Your ears be attentive to hear Your servant's prayer that I now pray to You day and night for Your servants, the Israelites. (Nehemiah 1:4, 6 NIV)

Before Nehemiah could stand in front of King Artaxerxes with his request for a leave of absence, he had to stand resolved before the God of heaven and fight for what mattered most on his knees. He had to stand with tenacity, fully trusting that his unshakable, omniscient God would equip and empower him for the task set before him.

One day in April, four months later, as I was serving the king his wine he asked me, "Why so sad? You aren't sick, are you? You look like a man with deep troubles." (For until then I had always been cheerful when I was with him.) I was badly frightened, but I replied, "Sir, why shouldn't I be sad? For the city where my ancestors are buried is in ruins, and the gates have been burned down."

"Well, what should be done?" the king asked.

With a quick prayer to the God of heaven, I replied, "If it please Your Majesty and if you look upon me with your royal favor, send me to Judah to rebuild the city of my fathers' graves, that I may rebuild it."

The king replied, with the queen sitting beside him, "How long will you be gone? When will you return?" So it was agreed! And I set a time for my departure! (Nehemiah 2:1–6 ESV)

Y'all, we can believe with confidence that what our God compels us to, commissions us to through compassion, and appoints with divinity, He will also equip!

It did please King Xeroxes to send Nehemiah. Moreover, it first pleased the King of Kings! God's purpose for the Israelites, and His provision for Nehemiah, is incredible!

First, a Persian king sitting on the throne should be hugely problematic, except that we read in Nehemiah 2:6 (NIV), "Then the king replied with the *queen* sitting beside him." This queen, sitting alongside the king, is believed to be none other than the Jewish-born Ester.[2] (For further study, read her story in the book of Esther.) Thanks to Queen Esther, Nehemiah found himself in the service of King Artaxerxes, who held a special place in his heart for the Jewish people. Incredible!

Second, the Israelites who were going home to Jerusalem were free to do so only because of what God did in and with King Cyrus of Persia.[3] In nine short years, Cyrus rose up an unapproachable empire and was strong enough to overtake Babylon and defeat King Nebuchadnezzar's successor. This ultimately ended up freeing the Israelites from captivity. All the amazing details concerning Cyrus were prophesized and foretold by the prophet Isaiah 150 years before coming to fruition! Our God is not random. He didn't miss one single detail providing for Nehemiah. God supplied Nehemiah with everything he would need for his task years before he would ever need it. Incredible! Once commissioned through compassion, once appointed to the task, this same God empowers us in the same extravagant way.

---

[2] Gail Wallace, "The Queen and the Cupbearer: Connections between Esther and Nehemiah." The Junia Project, 2015, http://juniaproject.com/queen-cupbearer-connections-esther-nehemiah.
[3] Christopher A. Rollston, "Nebuchadnezzar's Destruction of Jerusalem, the Cyrus Cylinder, and the Building of the Second Temple." Rollston Epigraphy, 2013, http://www.rollstonepigraphy.com/?p=544.

Reflect and Respond

When our hearts and the heart of the King of Kings agree, we can't imagine the power released to accomplish His purpose. There is no need to be afraid to humbly approach Him about what burdens your heart today.

Fight

Ask the King of heaven to extinguish any fear rising up at the thought of your appointment. Humbly approach your King, discuss what pleases Him concerning your personal commission (big or small), and clearly seek His purpose to accomplish the task. Fight for courage to make a difference—on your knees!

Build

Make a list of requirements you feel necessary for the job God has placed upon your heart, ask Him to supply you abundantly, and ask that you will not miss a single detail of His provision.

Day Seven

My Appointment with Distraction

Today's scripture reading: Nehemiah 2:7–8

My husband had surgery a while back, and as the nurses prepared to take him to the operating room, they directed me to a nearby waiting area, promising the doctor would find me in a couple of hours. Not wanting to eat or drink in front of my man prior to his surgery, I was hungry, and I needed coffee! Thankfully, there was a little café on the other side of the large waiting area. While standing in line and scanning the menu, a lady in front of me turned and said, "You can go on ahead of me; I don't even know what I want." I noticed a heaviness in her voice and saw a dullness in her eyes. I couldn't tell whether she was sick or just tired. I took her up on her offer and ordered my quiche and coffee. With my laptop over my shoulder, I scoped out a quiet corner in which to spend the next two hours, intent on working while I waited. I spotted the perfect little nook and placed my things down on a glass table in front of a small loveseat. After locating an electrical outlet behind me, I plugged in my laptop cord and turned just in time to see the woman from the line sitting down in my perfect spot. Now, that was irritating! I pulled the side table in front of a nearby chair to serve as a desk, and after setting my coffee on the floor and placing the quiche in my lap, I finally began to work.

However, I kept being distracted by the woman in my perfect spot because she sat there, staring, not texting, taking no phone calls, and doing nothing. The volume of her silence was deafening. I didn't want to be distracted, so I did what any good Christian woman would do: I simply turned my back toward her, shifting this lady in my perfect spot directly behind my right shoulder and out of sight. After all, I was busy and anxious about many things—good things, important things. I made a good effort to focus on my work.

About this time, the doctor found me and told me my husband's surgery went "better than expected," that my husband would be "good as new," and that after an hour or so, when he was out of recovery, a nurse would escort me back to be with him.

"Well, praise the Lord for good news! This went more quickly than expected," I said aloud as the doctor quickly walked away.

Ending her trance, the woman I had been attempting to ignore startled me by responding, "Yes, ma'am, praise the Lord indeed!" She continued, :Good as new. Now, wouldn't that be something?"

I nodded but didn't make eye contact, and I tried to remain focused. I tried to disregard her comment but could not; something had changed. As I looked back over my shoulder, I was suddenly struck to my core with compassion for this stranger. As hard as I had tried to redirect my focus, I was compelled by the Holy Spirit to stop and connect. After turning toward this hollow-eyed woman, I asked, "Do you have someone you're' waiting on?"

"Oh, yes, my husband, but I'm used to waiting on him." I saw a light switch on in her eyes. Smiling, she proudly declared, "We've been married forty-six years!"

"Wow, you have us beat by three years. What is your husband having done?"

"Well, this time he is getting his shunt changed. His port is getting infected, so they're putting a tube in his arm—for his dialysis."

"Oh, is there something wrong with his kidneys?"

"Yes, ma'am, there is … He doesn't have any." She told me details of his six-year battle with cancer, which was taking his organs and would eventually take his life "If God doesn't do a miracle."

"Oh, He can," I said. "I've seen Him do it in my own husband's life."

I shared with her my husband's story and how he'd gone from dead man walking to a walking miracle man almost twelve years ago.

As women do, we talked. We talked about our husbands, our children, and "those grandbabies." We shared our secret for getting a good scald on skillet-fried chicken. We shared our laughter, our hopes, our faith, and our encouragement right there in our perfect little spot.

"Your husband's procedure is finished," we heard the doctor say. She could back to see him now.

"I sure do thank you for visiting with me. It made the time pass," she said while gathering her things. "This has been a good blessing. God is good—you know it. Sunday, we should both get up and testify about our good God! You did say you go to church, right?"

"Oh, yes, ma'am, every chance I get," I said. "It keeps my husband happy because he is the pastor."

We laughed. While standing, it seemed appropriate to hug, so we did so. I asked her for her name and the name of her husband. "Leona and Leo," she said. "What's yours?"

"Ginger and Jimmy. I'll be praying for you two, Leona."

"Oh, I'll be praying for you too, girl."

As I look back on that day in the hospital, I can't help but think that this woman's still, somber focus was far from empty. Instead, I think she was going before the presence of the King of Kings in the middle of a hospital, and in the middle of a hospital, the Holy Spirit saturated me with compassion. At that moment, He handed me my appointment card and equipped me with overwhelming empathy for the task. I heard Him clearly speak into my spirit, "Ginger, encourage this woman for Me. She is a little down today. Give her some much-needed companionship and a mental timeout from her burdens."

While sitting in that waiting room, I had a choice: to either accept my divine appointment or keep working. I can give a ton of excuses for saying, "No, thanks, Lord." Overwhelmed, overworked, and overworried, I could have allowed myself to numb up, zone out emotionally, and let compassion fatigue have its way with me. I know God would have taken care of my sister in Christ, even if it meant giving the assignment to someone else, but I'm so thankful I listened to His leading. I saw an incredible blessing of God at work right before my eyes.

Empowered by the love of the Holy Spirit, I couldn't help but act, and God blessed, refreshed, and refurbished us both.

Reflect and Respond

We can't give from a depleted account; compassion fatigue is real. In our day of information overload, we can become so inundated with the pain and suffering of the world that we may feel helpless to affect any change. As Nehemiah prayed over his appointment from God, he took note and humbly but boldly took his supply list to King Artaxerxes. While you sit in your personal waiting room, wherever this may be, I want you to know that at just the right time, God will call. Don't be anxious—be encouraged! You can rest assured that whom He appoints and commissions, He will equip, and whom He equips, He will fully empower.

Fight

Practicing self-compassion on a regular basis is crucial. Begin caring for yourself, my friend, so you may be used to care for others.

This week, schedule the following.

- Write a list of your personal needs and then take them before the King.
- Pamper yourself a little. This week, do one thing you love but never allow yourself. Take care of your body even if you don't feel like it.
- Laugh every day this week.
- Make a gratitude list. Write out at least ten things for which you are especially blessed and thankful.

Build

I realize your God-given commission is probably not something about which you regularly think. Starting today, why not be intentional in asking God about your commission? Ask Him not to pass you by when He is handing out compassion appointments. Ask Him to break your heart for what breaks His. Ask Him to empower you to pick up your hammer and sword and fight for what matters so that you can help build what will last in your heart, in your home, in your community, and in your world.

Conclusion

Resurrecting Roosters

I need to tell you the rest of the rooster story.

That next morning in the cabin, I finally gathered up enough nerve to peel back the butcher paper that hugged my wounded rooster. To my surprise, he was still completely intact. However, the impressive lid expanding from neck to tail didn't fare as well. I couldn't stop the gasp escaping my lips as I watched it spill out in hundreds of pieces onto the table. Several months later, my sweet husband spent many hours meticulously bonding those pieces back together. The lid is now fully repaired and restored to its proper place upon the rooster's back. Oh, there is certainly a chip here and there, and he bares many glue seam scars. My rooster is never going to be as good as new, but he turned out better than expected because now he sits at the center of a far better story. Each time I look at my rooster, his story reminds me of the following.

- Love is far from perfect, but it's perfectly shameless in its worthy pursuit
- Love cares, love acts, and love does
- Love binds things together
- Love mends

We are a fragile, resilient, imperfect people, fully restored and reestablished only through the relentless love of Christ. It is His love that binds us all together, and it is His love in us that demands compassion from us. He alone allows us to see the broken pieces that need to be mended in this hurting world. It is God, through Christ Jesus, who compels us by the power of the Holy Spirit to be the answer on the other side of the desperate prayers of the brokenhearted.

This is Nehemiah's testimony, his story. Nehemiah lived a life on the other side of prayer. The Israelites had prayed hard, fast, and continuously for the wall to be rebuilt. This wall meant security, order, and restoration of a sovereign, self-governed state, but more important, it meant rescuing a nation of people from despair. The people prayed, God commissioned, Jesus equipped, and the Holy Spirit empowered. Nehemiah said, "If it please the King" (Nehemiah 2:5 NIV), and he built the wall in fifty-two days! Nehemiah never knew, this side of heaven, the amazing impact of his finished appointment, but we sure do. From this restored people, out from the line of David almost five hundred years later, came the most important appointment of all time: our Jesus said yes to His God-given commission. His empathy and love for a hurting world took Him all the way to the cross.

Now, that is compassion. Where will your compassion take you?

What a wonderful Savior!

Hallelujah, and pass the tissue.

Week Two

Living in Community

Day One

Friendship and Community

While walking the halls at an elementary school, this time as a mom, I am keenly aware that the whole mean girl syndrome hasn't changed. I am not talking about the girls on the playground. I am talking about PTA meetings, field trips, and even the car pickup line. I never dreamed that as an adult, making friends could cause me to feel like that insecure middle-school girl all over again.

The word *friend* conjures up all sorts of emotions, doesn't it? There are emotions that are good and sweet, but there is also fear, betrayal, insecurity, and even apathy. Being a friend is not for the faint of heart. Yet God has revealed to me that I must face all these emotions because relationships, friendships, and community are the primary tools He uses to empower His children for their callings.

Yes, I do understand the desire to remain emotionally isolated—the idea of having friends yet being guarded and not allowing them to know you deeply. But when we refuse to engage with others in a deep and meaningful way, we are playing into Satan's schemes and hindering the work of God in our lives.

A quick post, tweet, or selfie on social media has taken the place of one-on-one conversations. Busyness has become an easy excuse for not engaging with others. Our insecurity speaks to our hearts and hides behind these false connections. The result is Christian women who are longing to be known, are thirsting for more, and are apathetic to the needs of others.

Proverbs 18:1 (HCSB) states it painfully clear: "One who isolates himself pursues selfish desires; (s)he rebels against all sound judgment."

I wholeheartedly believe the busyness epidemic in our culture is a ploy by Satan to hinder God's people from enjoying the bounty and power of God within the Christian community. Satan knows that we are stronger together.

The Bible teaches that when believers gather,

- our prayers are heard (Malachi 3:16),
- the presence of God dwells among us (Matthew 18:20),
- life is better together (Psalms 133:1), and
- we can fight off temptation (Ecclesiastes 4:10).

This week, ladies, is not about getting a new bestie (although you might gain one). It's about embracing the Christian women God has placed in your life. This week, we are diving into the topic of building Christian community. God brings us together—widows, young moms, empty nesters, college girls, divorcees, singles, late nighters, and early risers. The saying "Opposites attract" is true when it comes to building community. A community that empowers is made up of women who are bonded not merely by their season but through the blood of Christ.

We will see all women can come together to experience God's full empowerment within the Christian community by living backward, living forward, and living side by side.

Reflect and Respond

We should strive to walk the halls this week not avoiding the mean girls but prayerfully seeking the community of women God has designed to bring life, strength, and joy into our lives. Life is not living if it is done alone. Empowerment is defined as becoming stronger and more confident, especially in claiming one's rights. As a child of God, you, dear daughter, are part of a family, so be empowered! Live in community with your family. It will bring confidence in yourself, in your God, and in His commissioning over your life.

Fight

Pause and pray. What emotions does the word *friend* conjure?

safety – life long – warm laughter

In what ways do you recognize resistance to building a stronger Christian community of women in your life?

margin sometimes think – I have no room

Ask God to specifically reveal areas of fear, excuses, and selfishness that might hold you back from this fellowship.

Build

Memorize Ecclesiastes 4:9–10. Praise God that He already knows the names of the women He will use to empower you over the next weeks, months, and years.

Day Two

Living Backward

A young woman was washed in the water of baptism at the age of twenty-five, and the salvation of Jesus Christ radically changed her life. She became a student of God's word and drank deeply of His wisdom. By age thirty-two, she taught small groups, had Bible studies in her home, and was a strong pillar of faith. At a glance, it appeared she was surrounded by a strong community within her local church. Though her friendships were genuine, she was guarded. Each time she drew near to a fellow sister in Christ, the whisper came: "Don't forget who you used to be. Remember what you have done." She shuddered at the thought of her past being discovered, and the wall around her heart would return. Isolated in her despair, her grief and shame would return year after year as she mourned the anniversary of her abortion alone.

Then one year, by God's providence, on the anniversary of the abortion, she bumped into a woman from church. This woman saw a sadness in the young woman's eyes she couldn't shake. Through gentle persistence, the guard around the young woman's heart came off, releasing sobs of utter brokenness. Sinking into the woman's embrace, she found no judgment, only arms of love that held her as they cried together. Her past had held her in bondage long enough. The young woman needed a friend to remind her that God had forgiven her, and with her friend's support, she could learn to forgive herself. Every year since that first confession to her friend, the young woman has not spent that date on the calendar alone. She and her friend spend it together, grieving the loss and celebrating the grace of God.

Therefore if anyone is in Christ, he is a new creation. The old has passed away; behold, the new has come. (2 Corinthians 5:17 ESV)

We see in the pages of Nehemiah another example of how overwhelming despair was defeated when believers rallied together.

And so I arrived in Jerusalem. After I had been there three days, I got up in the middle of the night, I and a few men who were with me. I hadn't told anyone what my God had put in my heart to do for Jerusalem. The only animal with us was the one I was riding. Under cover of night I went past the Valley Gate toward the Dragon's Fountain to the Dung Gate looking over the walls of Jerusalem, which had been broken through and whose gates had been burned up. I then crossed to the Fountain Gate and headed for the King's Pool but there wasn't enough room for the donkey I was riding to get through. So, I went up the valley in the dark continuing my inspection of the wall. I came back in through the Valley Gate. The local officials had no idea where I'd gone or what I was doing—I hadn't breathed a word to the Jews, priests, nobles, local officials, or anyone else who would be working on the job. Then I gave them my report: "Face it: we're in a bad way here. Jerusalem is a wreck; its gates are burned up. Come—let's build the wall of Jerusalem and not live with this disgrace any longer." I told them how God was supporting me and how the king was backing me up. They said, "We're with you. Let's get started." They rolled up their sleeves, ready for the good work. (Nehemiah 2:11–18 The Message)

Overwhelmed by the magnitude of destruction and past failed attempts to rebuild the wall, the nation of Israel sat in ruin. Without a wall, the people were vulnerable to enemies, the temple was exposed, and homes could not be built. Life was on hold due to the rubble. Nehemiah cast the vision of a united people tackling the overwhelming task together. Overcoming our past and current sins is hard work, but it doesn't have to be lonely work.

To build community, we must first live backward. We live backward by acknowledging and owning our rubble, our past sin, bondage, brokenness, and ruin. *Ruin* is a strong word, implying utter destruction. At times, as we survey our lives, we will find a portion of the wall beginning to crumble or perhaps a gate hanging on its hinges. At other times, we find destruction and ruin. Either way, we all have rocks on the ground that hinder the movement of God in our lives. Nehemiah described Israel's ruin as a disgrace to God. Ladies, God is not disgraced by you, but if we live life without allowing Him to rebuild those areas of rubble, then our testimonies will be a disgrace because He is not a God of ruin but a God of restoration.

Reflect and Respond

Shame is our first thought when we consider past or current sins. Confessing a sin is acknowledging to God that you agree it is wrong, but Satan uses our shame to hold us in bondage. Romans 8:1 (HCSB) states, "Therefore, no condemnation now exists for those in Christ Jesus." Satan wants to condemn, but the Holy Spirit brings about conviction that leads to repentance and restoration.

Believers need to celebrate with their community when Christ brings freedom from sins. We need to lock arms with each other and be honest when we are battling temptation. Growing in the Lord takes a community. Community offers accountability, wisdom, and hope. Whatever it is you have done or are struggling with, there is another woman within your community who has been redeemed and is living in victory from that area of rubble. You need her guidance and support, and you need to see what freedom looks like in her life. Living backward teaches us to take our focus off the rubble and put it on the One who rebuilds.

We are a community of sinners who live in victory. We connect through our rubble, not our perfections. As you pick up your hammer to build community, the enemy will whisper, "Do you really belong?" Sister, Christ's blood answered that question once and for all! If the voice of condemnation has stalled your life, today is the day you need to start fighting back. We're with you.

Fight

Resist the urge to hide your rubble and show only the "pretty" side of life. Write about a time that the voice of condemnation trapped you.

Was or is that voice your own, or the voice of others?

How did or does that voice compound your anxiety to reach out in areas of weakness?

Build

What victory have you experienced that someone else needs to hear?

Reach out to someone who is walking a road you know, and encourage them today. (Examples: a fellow widow, a single parent, singleness, a job loss, an addiction, a recent move, loss of a parent.)

Day Three

The Sabbath and Community

One Sunday after church, we had two families over for a casual lunch. It was so causal, in fact, that they ended up helping us finish the cooking because the roast decided to revolt. These sweet friends didn't mind. We laughed, ate a smorgasbord, and then busted out some games—a round of Catch Phrase, Uno, and 5 Seconds. They stayed all day. When dinnertime rolled around, one of the dads said to his daughter, "This is what Sundays used to look like." We enjoyed laughter and chasing kids, and the men enjoyed a little golf on TV. After they left, his words still rang in my ears. It had been a true Sabbath.

In Nehemiah 8:15–17, we see when the people began to fill the city of Jerusalem, they devoted time to listening to the law of the Lord. Within the scrolls of scripture, they found instructions they had neglected. With joyful obedience, they started following God's commands.

> So they proclaimed and spread this news throughout their towns and in Jerusalem, saying, "Go out to the hill country and bring back branches of olive, wild olive, myrtle, palm, and other leafy trees to make booths, just as it is written." The people went out, brought back branches, and made booths for themselves on each of their rooftops, and courtyards, the court of the house of God, the square by the Water Gate, and the square by the Gate of Ephraim. The whole community that had returned from exile made booths and lived in them. They had not celebrated like this from the days of Joshua son of Nun until that day. And there was tremendous joy. (Nehemiah 8:15–17 HCSB)

Society tells us God's law is restrictive and rigorous, and if you are having fun, it must be a sin. However, in reality the only time we will experience deep, lasting joy is when we are living in accordance to God's law. I love that our God likes festivals! He commands His people to gather together, eat, celebrate, remember, and worship Him. This weeklong celebration the Israelites practiced released a joy within the people that had been missing in their worship and in the rhythms of daily life. How good is our God?

Spending time in fellowship with other believers is worshiping our God. Mathew 22:37–40 (HCSB) instructs us to "Love the Lord your God with all your heart, with all your soul, and with all your mind. This is the greatest and most important command. The second is like it: Love your neighbor as yourself. All the Law and the Prophets depend on these two commands."

When Jesus says, "The second is like it," He is saying the two are connected: you cannot fully love God if you do not love His family. We will experience God's full empowerment when we choose to live side by side. Simply put, living side by side is letting others into the daily rhythms of life. God's family is diverse, so we will most likely be building relationships with different women in different seasons. My personal community of ladies includes women in their eighties down to their teens. Each of these women teaches me, encourages me, challenges me, and brings joy to my heart.

The people of Jerusalem didn't know they were supposed to build booths and celebrate in such a manner. However, as soon as they heard what they were supposed to do, they excitedly spread the news and included everyone. When we gather with our sisters, we are going to chat about the daily things: marriage, kids, homework, housework, weight, food, sleep, health. Those are issues we are celebrating or battling, but it is also crucial that we speak about God and what we are learning or where we are doubting. The joy of community comes when we are seeking God together.

That Sunday at my house, we had nine kids, six adults, and one dog. Yes, we worked, juggled, made messes, and picked them up. But when I say it was a true Sabbath, I mean we rested in the presence of one another and in the common love of Christ. We worshiped our God together, and then we feasted and celebrated together. Okay, feast may be an exaggeration for what we actually ate that day. Nonetheless, God blessed our hearts because we were observing His laws by living side by side.

Reflect and Respond

Relationships take time. They take awkward moments and uncomfortable conversations until one day you leave each other's presence feeling as though you just spent time with family. Those sweet couples from my story have been in our lives for over six years. Slowly, over dinners, Bible studies, prayer requests shared in church, playdates, phone calls, and texts, our relationships have deepened.

Give yourself grace as you reach out and begin to build new relationships. Be patient with others by not setting expectations on them. Simply offer an invitation and start living life side by side, watching as God begins to knit hearts together.

Fight

Part of the empowerment God brings through community is freedom for sisters in Christ to share how God is moving in their lives. Write about a time you have experienced a deep joy from sharing with another woman the things God was teaching you or doing in your life.

Focus on how that conversation spurred you on in your relationship with God.

Build

Over the next week, as you engage with other Christian women, steer the conversation to the things of God. Plan a time to live side by side with a sister in Christ and then come back and reflect on that time.

- Did it make you nervous?
- Did conversation flow?
- Were you able to talk freely about the things of God?
- Was your heart encouraged when you left?

Day Four

Bad Advice

Well-meaning people offer bad advice all the time. I have been guilty of this; haven't you? However, a friend offering bad advice without ill intentions is altogether different from someone purposefully seeking to speak harm into our lives. We need to be keenly aware of the people whom we allow to influence our lives. Acknowledging those whose words have power over our thoughts, self-image, confidence, decision making, spiritual growth, marriages, and parenting is vital. In Nehemiah 6, we see that Sanballat, Tobiah, and Geshem were trying to persuade Nehemiah to meet with them. He was aware they were his enemies and wanted to distract him from finishing the work God had set before him. He refused to allow their words to influence his decisions. However, after that refusal, the voice of someone more trusted came along. Read about this encounter in Nehemiah 6:10–13.

> I went to the house of Shemaiah son of Delaiah, son of Mehetabel, who was restricted to his house. He said: Let us meet at the house of God inside the temple. Let us shut the temple doors because they are coming to kill you. They are coming to kill you tonight! But I said, "Should a man like me run away? How can I enter the temple and live? I will not go." I realized that God had not sent him, because of the prophecy he spoke against me. Tobiah and Sanballat had hired him. He was hired, so that I would be intimidated, do as he suggested, sin, and get a bad reputation, in order that they could discredit me. (Nehemiah 6:10–13 HCSB)

The sting of deception hurts. My heart knows that pain, and I am sure yours does too. We have all been blindsided by a "friend" whose intentions were not for our good. Perhaps the pain caused us to hesitate in building community. Allowing others to truly know us gives them the opportunity to deeply wound us, but, sister, don't let fear hold you back from experiencing the empowerment God is yearning to pour into your life through community. We will build our community with eyes wide open, just like Nehemiah. We need to have a keen, discerning spirit to recognize the Sanballats, Tobiahs, and Geshems in our lives, the people who are openly against God's movements. We also need a discerning spirit for those who wear the face of a friend yet oppose the work God is doing in us.

I would love to tell you that if you build a community of Christian women, you will never feel this sting, but David reminds us that even those in God's family are not exempt. In Psalm 55:12–14 (HCSB), we read about the pain he felt: "Now it is not an enemy who insults me—otherwise I could bear it; it is not a foe who rises up against me—otherwise I could hide from him. But it is you, a man who is my peer, my companion and good friend! We used to have close fellowship; we walked with the crowd into the house of God." So why am I pleading with you to build community yet warning you about the possibility of betrayal? I don't want you to be blindsided. We are building a community that empowers, and that, sister, will bring about some resistance. God's movements have enemies.

Did you notice how, in the passage from Nehemiah, as soon as Nehemiah sensed his "friend's" words were a ploy to destroy the work of God, he immediately left? We don't get a glimpse into his thoughts, so don't take this as scholarly interpretation, but from the directness of his words and his immediate return to work, I am inclined to say Nehemiah recognized the man as a liar, traitor, and distracter. Nehemiah didn't sit in the wound of deception; he realized the problem was with Shemaiah, and he didn't take it personally. He knew the attack was against God and God's work. As women, we love deeply, and therefore we wound deeply. If someone you trust tries to derail you from God's work, move on, sister! Don't let it swallow you emotionally. Acknowledge it as an attack on the movement of God, not on you personally. We must focus on the calling and guard the work. We build with those who are for us and ignore the voice of those who aren't.

Reflect and Respond

Ladies, as we build our community, we must be aware of the advice we are receiving. Is it good, godly advice? Is it well-meaning advice? Is the advice meant to derail the work of God? We protect ourselves from betrayal by evaluating the amount of influence others have in our lives. We must keep all our relationships in balance and rely on the Lord's Word as our final and most impactful voice.

Fight

How much weight do the opinions and advice of others hold over your decisions? Is there someone whose opinion you hold highly? How might this affect what God is asking you to build?

parents husband

Build

Hebrews 5:14 (HCSB) states, "But solid food is for the mature—for those whose senses have been trained to distinguish between good and evil." Discernment is needed to recognize those who seek to stop the work. We must know the voice of God to distinguish between the truth and the lies. Do you have a daily or a weekly method to put God's Word, His true and always good advice, into your heart? If not, write out your plan. Remember to be practical, simple, and realistic; there's no need to get fancy here! Before you start on your plan, remind yourself what Psalm

1:1–3 says: "Blessed is the man who walks not in the counsel of the wicked, nor stands in the way of sinners, nor sits in the seat of scoffers; but his delight is in the law of the Lord, and on his law, he meditates day and night. He is like a tree planted by streams of water that yields its fruit in its season, and its leaf does not wither. Whatever he does prospers."

Day Five

Living, Listening, Loving

A friend invited several of us over to show off her new home, and she worked hard to get it ready for us. I did not have time in my schedule for a playdate, yet it was important to her, so it was important to me to be supportive. The kids ran wild as the moms tried to talk and keep the house new. During our conversation, I mentioned I should be at home cleaning my own house because the weekend was approaching, and I had company coming. I shared how I had no clue how I was going to make the house sparkle when my schedule was at a max.

A few days later, I received a text asking, "Is your house clean?" As my eyes surveyed the house, the answer was an overwhelming no. The following text said, "I am coming over. I will bring my cleaning supplies." This sweet friend had picked up on the fact that in this season of my life, in this week, I needed help with a house that seemed all-consuming.

What this friend didn't know is in reality, Satan has an easy target when I am overwhelmed with daily motherly duties. He is sure to tell me so, "You can't even keep up, so why would God be able to do any more with you?" Then my own heart whispers, "You can't work, teach at church, continue with Worthy Pursuit Ministries, and be a good mother. Look, you can't even …" The list goes on. So because I listened to the lies that day, I didn't allow my friend to come. I called her and said, "Oh, no …" She tried persuading me, so I promised if I didn't get it done that evening, then she could come help me the next morning.

I would not have let my own mother in my house, let alone a new friend! You see, I was raised that when people come over, the house should be clean. Now, as a momma with three kids, I'm fine with tidy. But that day, the house was embarrassing. Truthfully, it was more than my messy house. I really didn't want her to see my rubble. Frankly, I was caught up in the myth of perfectionism. I convinced myself I had to be someone who always has her house (and life) sparkling. After all, what would she think of me if she saw my mess? Perfectionism, pride, and embarrassment stole a blessing from both me and my friend that day.

When a friend makes an offer to help, how often do we reply, "No, thank you"? We don't need a meal, help with the kids, or someone to go to the doctor appointment with us. We don't ask whether we can join someone for dinner or admit we need help reading our Bible. We struggle alone and end up feeling isolated and overwhelmed, all the while politely refusing help. We are told we can achieve it all as highly capable women, yet our hearts are aching with the reality that we can't—not alone.

Living empowered in Christ will require side-by-side living that listens and chooses to live forward together with love. We must be willing to allow others into the daily rhythms of our lives, which—let's be real— isn't always in tune, on beat, or even upbeat! The beauty of my friend is while she was living beside me, she listened to more than my words. She heard my need. She was willing to jump into the middle of my life no matter what it looked like.

She wasn't asking that I have it all together; she was offering to be part of the solution to my current problem. Insecurity held me back from accepting her gift of victory that day.

The façade of perfectionism is stealing empowerment from our daily living. Remember, it's in our weakness where Christ strength shows through. Often it is our community that demonstrates His power during weak moments of our lives. When we allow ourselves to be vulnerable, friendships are formed and relationships deepen.

> Then I said to the nobles, the officials, and the rest of the people: "The work is enormous and spread out, and we are separated far from one another along the wall.

Wherever you hear the trumpet sound, rally to us there. Our God will fight for us!" (Nehemiah 4:19–20 HCSB)

Living in community provides an opportunity for others to hear your trumpet sounding. The grind of life can wear on our resolve, our focus, our joy. We can begin to feel spread out and separated. We need to be Christian sisters who are vulnerable enough to sounds our trumpets, and we need sisters who listen for the trumpet of others. I have a woman in my life who, on multiple occasions, says, "I can see that overwhelmed look in your eyes." Each time she has come to me, I have been blind to the condition of my own spirit, but when I pause to reflect on her words, I realize she is right. She is a tangible reminder that it is okay to admit when our faith is faltering, our spirits are broken, and our hearts are confused. It's okay to show more than just the pretty side of life. Living side by side means living forward with God's strength, listening for the call from others, and being brave enough to sound the trumpet for ourselves.

Reflect and Respond

You can probably name ten people who are fighting a battle today. If they put down their hammers to pick up their swords alone, they are in danger of never getting back to the work for which God has called them. We rally to our sisters in Christ so we can hold the sword and fight back against the enemy. We battle against the pressures of life, the lies, and the doubt, and we replace those things with hope, joy, laughter, and the freedom of meaningful connection. We fight by offering a word of encouragement with the prompting of the Holy Spirit; a text, phone call, lunch, or a card in the mail makes a ripple that lasts for eternity. Even though I refused the physical help of my friend joining me to clean my home, God used that text conversation to snap me out of a destructive cycle. I devised a plan to stop the chaos and the negative self-talk, and to fix the root of the problem. We never know how much our small act of love can really do when God is at the heart of it. Do not be afraid to sound that trumpet; it will make you stronger. Rally for your sisters; don't let them lay their hammers aside. Live forward together.

Fight

Why is it hard for you to ask and/or receive help when others offer? Do you have a stigma around the idea of sounding your trumpet?

Build

What sister needs you to rally to her this week?

Is she sounding her trumpet and asking for help, or do you simply feel the prompting of the Spirit?

What is one action you can take to show her love?

After you have completed this act of love, write about the result.

Day Six

Friendship and Community

Today's scripture reading: Nehemiah 4:6

It is a sacred thing, therefore, to take a new friend into our lives. We accept a solemn responsibility when we do so. We do not know what burdens we may be assuming, what sacrifices we may, unconsciously, be pledging ourselves to make, what sorrows may come to us through the one to whom we are opening our heart. We should choose our friends, therefore, thoughtfully, wisely, prayerfully—but when we have pledged our love, we should be faithful, whatever the cost may be!

—J. R. Miller

I went through a season thinking I didn't have time for deeper community. I kept my friendships informal, free of any commitment or expectations. I have a wonderful family, and that is enough for me. I even went so far as to label myself a bad friend. I had decided that being a friend was not a spiritual gift God had given to me. Friends took too much work and invited drama into life. I was happy with surface level relationships; that was all I had time for and all I needed.

During this season in my life, God moved a childhood friend across the street from me and my husband. We were so excited to catch up. We borrowed sugar and eggs from one another, had impromptu lunches and dinners, went on long walks when we fought with our new husbands, and searched for runaway dogs on more occasions then I can count. She ran over when she found out she was pregnant, and she delivered yellow roses and held me tightly when I had my first miscarriage. We met in the middle of the road and bawled when her father passed away. We lived life together through the good days, the bad days, the happy days, and the hard days. We talked scripture, swapped recipes, and didn't apologize for our personal crazy.

Then without warning, God moved her twelve hours away. Our conversations on the phone were interrupted by kids, work, and life, but we kept at it. God had brought this woman, who is a naturally good friend, into my life, and I learned thoughtfulness from her. He placed her across the street so I couldn't run from the calling of community, and He used her gifts to draw me out of solitude, hiding, and denial. He used her gifts to show me the value of Christian community!

> So we rebuilt the wall until the entire wall was joined together up to half its height, for the people had the will to keep working. (Nehemiah 4:6 HSCB)

The will to continue building a community is part of the work. There will be days that you are exhausted emotionally, mentally, and physically as a result of reaching out and loving others. Remember, one of my major hang-ups is my labeling myself as a bad friend. Truthfully, I am not naturally thoughtful. I am horrible at remembering birthdays, special needs, or anniversaries of loved ones who have passed. I am horrible about checking in and keeping up with people. You may recognize yourself in the description above. If so, let me share with you the result of my confession. God brought my sweet friend into my life to show me opposite of all my ways. She is thoughtful to a fault and remembers birthdays. God taught me that I need to be disciplined to make time to show love. Just as I do things in a marriage that speak my husband's language of love, I need to purposefully do things that speak love to those God has purposefully brought into my community.

Being part of the family of God is a sacred gift.

Reflect and Respond

Do you have the will to keep working at friendships, mentorships, and relationships? Love is a verb, and as you build your community, God will reveal natural habits that need to be redeemed to better reflect His image. Don't fear, sister, if you are more like me than you'd care to admit. God can teach us both how to be good friends. In fact, it's one of my favorite journeys that He has taken me on so far.

Fight

Do you consider yourself to be a good friend to others? If so, why? If not, why?

Build

I am going to ask you to be vulnerable. Remember that being part of God's family is not something to take lightly. We are to strive for empowerment by the Holy Spirit and continued growth in Christ, and sometimes that requires us to hear the truth from someone who loves us.

- Ask close friends, a spouse, or family members if they consider you to be loyal and/or thoughtful. Write down the answers.

- Ask them to tell you your strengths as a friend, and one area in which you might grow. Write down the answer.

Pray that your heart will not be defensive. Be humbled and willing to accept their honest perspective. For you, I pray, "Holy Spirit, be with my sisters so that they may build a community that empowers them and releases the full joy of Christ into their lives."

Day Seven

Empowerment and Community

The first of the Israelites, who had been exiled, returned to their homeland over one hundred years prior to the events written in the book of Nehemiah. This was not the Israelites' first attempt to rebuild the wall. Their enemies assumed they would fail again, just as in previous times. However, God had a plan to restore His people, and He has a plan to restore you! God has a purpose for your life, and that purpose is to make an impact for His kingdom. You can choose to pursue His purposes solo and build alone, but if you do, it will be a long, hard, lonely struggle.

The good news for us is the Israelites did succeed! The wall was built, and it was done in record time. But they didn't do it solo. What they accomplished together shows us when the body of Christ locks arms for a specific purpose, God covers the project with His power, and then He receives the glory! Nehemiah confirms it is possible to fight for what is right. We can build what lasts. We can live victoriously by the empowerment of the Holy Spirit within a community together—brick by brick, person by person, conversation by conversation, prayer by prayer, encouragement by encouragement, confession by confession—as iron sharpening iron for God's glory!

Empowerment is what we want. It's what we need! We want to experience the living God within the daily routines of life. We want to drink of the living water and thirst no more (John 4:13–14). We not only want to witness the active hand of God in our day to day, but we want to be part of His everyday miracles. We desire that our marriages go from surviving to thriving, that our children laugh more than they sass, and that our families be firmly rooted in the knowledge of scripture. We desire to make a difference in our work, homes, and community; we want our lives to matter. We want the laundry to fold itself, the dinner to cook itself, and the groceries to get put away without us. Okay, wait, maybe I am getting carried away ...

Seriously, though, sometimes we lump our spiritual dreams in with the wishes we have about nominal daily tasks. The difference is our spiritual dreams are actual promises from a supreme God. They are not fictional wishes but actual possibilities.

We can all experience God's full empowerment.

Stop and say that out loud: "I can experience God's full empowerment."

Do you believe that?

Reflect and Respond

We can all experience God's full empowerment within a Christian community. Nehemiah had a God-sized vision. God brought the people together to accomplish the task and knit back the community to His original intention. Ask God to put a vision for community in your heart. As He grows this desire within you, He will bring women with whom He wants you to go through life. Be open to His leading, remembering that opposites help sharpen us and diversity causes us to see more of Christ. I have experienced the beauty of this empowerment and gift that God has provided, and I know that your life will be so much sweeter because you have chosen to gather with other women and share, laugh, cry, and eat through the seasons that come!

Fight

Review what the following scriptures say about what happens when we are in community.

- Our prayers are heard (Malachi 3:16)
- The presence of God dwells among us (Matthew 18:20)
- Life is better together (Psalm 133:1)
- We can fight temptation (Ecclesiastes 4:9–10)

Build

Which of the benefits above do you need right now in something to which God has called you?

If you have a Christian community supporting you, how are you currently seeing the truth of this in your life?

How is your calling being hindered because you are lacking the power that comes through community?

Conclusion

Call to Community

We have spent this week talking about weaving a community of Christian women into the everyday fabric of your life. Building up a wall of relationships to protect you spiritually as you live backward facing your rubble, live side by side while rearranging your priorities and your calendar, and accepting the challenge to act in love.

My heart's cry is that the Holy Spirit will move you toward a solid Christian community and that He will soften your heart toward others so that you in turn reach out. Sister, empowerment is confidence in your calling. The tasks God calls us to will make our knees weak. However, as members of a community, we have others to support us, encourage us, pray over us, and propel us into the life God created us to walk in for the increase of his kingdom.

God's empowerment is not reserved for a few special people. It is freely given to all who call upon His name. However, the difference between those who have His empowerment and those who do not is their level of obedience.

Pick up you hammer, sister. Enjoy this journey.

God created us for relationships according to Genesis 2:18, and in His grace, He gave us this beautiful bond with fellow believers that is unexplainable yet pure joy.

Week Three

Fighting Opposition

Day One

Challenge Accepted!

The book of Nehemiah is a powerful story of one man daring to obey God no matter the cost. This man accepts a call from God to resurrect victory from ruin. Nehemiah stands firm to rally his entire nation, the Israelites, despite the opposition. His faith in God provides courage to stand up and fight for what matters most, and to build what lasts, for God's glory.

This bold and victorious leader sets out to obey God and not only build a wall but restore God's people in the process. Along the way, he encounters great opposition. Nations invade, attempting to derail Nehemiah and stop his people from doing the work God commissioned them to do. Opposition came not only from outside the city walls but also from within. His own nation tries to discourage Nehemiah through lies, deceit, and corruption. In fact, from the moment Nehemiah announces his call by God to lead the nation of Israel in rebuilding the wall, his enemies came against him from all sides.

Nehemiah never gives up! He never lets trials and tribulations overcome him as he walks obediently with His God. He walked in faith day in and day out. And guess what? At the end, he looked up and saw an incredible wall erected to full height and strength, just as God had promised. Was it hard? Absolutely! Did Nehemiah and the people want to give up? Yes! Yet they kept their faith in the One who would go before them, sustain them, and empower them to accomplish all God asked.

God doesn't need a massive army to win a battle against the enemy. He simple needs one individual who will chose to be empowered by the

Holy Spirit and walk in obedience! Will that be you, my friend? Will you dare to obey what God is calling you to build? Will you dare to fight no matter what obstacles get in your way? I pray it is! Your God will fight for you and for me when we simply obey His call.

But in order for us to obey, we have to know how to fight our opponent. You may say, "*Our* opponent? You mean you and I have an enemy just like Nehemiah?" Yes! This enemy tries to knock down any God-size wall we are building. He tries to knock us off our feet, hoping we never get back up. He doesn't play fair, and he doesn't give up because you have had enough.

Your enemy would like nothing more than to see your marriage crumble and fall, see your children live wayward lives, see a nation denounce their heritage of obeying God, see a struggling single mom give up the fight, see a young girl surrender her purity outside of marriage, see a mom live in loneliness and shame, and see her children miss the rearing God intend.

This enemy doesn't care how he hurts you or me. His ultimate goal is to hurt God, and the best way to hurt the loving Father is to hurt His children.

If we want to be the one woman who moves on behalf of our God, we have to learn to fight, ladies! Fight back against our enemy!

Buckle up, my friend, because over the next few days, we are going to learn how we can pick up our swords to defend and fight back against the opposition trying to stop us. We will learn the tactics Satan uses, discover where we are the weakest so we can make a plan to defend it, and become empowered to stand up against whatever our enemy throws at us.

No longer will we be women unaware or unprepared for the battle at hand. We will be mighty warriors! We will be women who are building what God has called us to, with a hammer in one hand and a sword in the other—and not just any sword, but a sharp and powerful sword. We are prepared to fight in God's army for the glory of His name!

Reflect and Respond

> The world has yet to see what God can do with a man fully consecrated to him. By God's help, I aim to be that man.
>
> —Dwight L. Moody

D. L. Moody, a great evangelist, decided to fully obey God and saw over a million people give their hearts to Christ. God brought revival to the souls of many people across two continents because of Moody's obedience to preach. He is one man who chose obedience no matter the cost. What could God do through you, and the lives of those around you, if you chose total obedience despite the cost?

Fight

Like Nehemiah, we often experience opposition as we try to do God's will. What is it that God has called you to? Is it worth fighting for?

What would happen if Satan prevented you from accomplishing your commission from God?

Build

How can you be more obedient to God today than you were yesterday? Ask God to reveal His will to you today.

As you listen for His voice, commit this day to obey no matter what obstacles get in your way (Joshua 24:15). Commit *before* the obstacle arises!

http://www.christianitytoday.com/history/issues/issue-25/world-has-yet-to-see.html
http://www.dailyintheword.org/rooted/what-god-can-do-with-a-surrendered-life

Day Two

Waking up with a Vengeance

Today's scripture reading: Nehemiah 4:11

The sun rises over the calm and tranquil ocean. A normal day begins—another perfect day in Hawaii. The sound of the ocean waves roll up on the sandy shores, creating a peaceful bliss.

Then suddenly life is interrupted. Bombs begin to explode, wiping out all things normal and peaceful. It is Sunday, December 7, 1941, and Japan successfully executes a surprise attack at Pearl Harbor, Hawaii. No one is ready for it, and the enemy gives a devastating blow.

Japan was a major enemy to the United States, but up until this point, the United States had not declared war. Therefore when the attack came, it truly was a surprise. That day 2,335 people were killed, 1,143 were wounded, twenty naval vessels sunk to the depths of the ocean (including eight enormous battleships), and three hundred airplanes were destroyed and shot down.

Had the United States been ready for the attack, there might not have been the massive devastation and lives lost. They could have prepared to fight and defend themselves from their enemy. Japan knew if the great United States was caught unaware, victory would be certain.

Today, I want you to think and pray about the war that is being waged against us, the army of God. It is a war that many of us are unaware of and unprepared for. Christians have an opponent that is out to "steal, kill and destroy us" (John 10:10 NIV), and Satan will swoop in with a surprise attack if we don't get ready! Perhaps he already has.

Becoming aware of the war that is raging against us and being prepared to fight against our enemy will equip us to withstand his tactics and help us win the battle!

For two long hours Japan, rained down bombs on US soil in hopes the American people would be disheartened and never join the war. Contrary to their hopes, the people of the United States rallied, and it has been said, what Japan really did that day in 1941 was wake a sleeping giant from its slumber. The United States woke up with a vengeance and fought like it had something worth fighting for—because it did.

When the women of God wake up to our enemy, declare war, and "fight for our country men, our sons and our daughters, our [husbands] and homes" (Nehemiah 4:14b HCSB), the enemy doesn't stand a chance! May we begin to step into the empowerment of the Holy Spirit we already possess and awaken the inner warrior within each of us.

Let's wake up, and not just to fear or the awareness of the battle. Let's wake up with a vengeance, knowing that our God wins in the end! We are on the winning side, and we definitely have something worth fighting for!

> Then our enemies said, "They won't know or see anything until we're among them and can kill them and stop the work." (Nehemiah 4:11 HCSB)

The words of the enemy became reality in the lives of the Israelites. They ran to Nehemiah for help, saying, "Everywhere you turn they attack us!" (Nehemiah 4:12 HCSB). Nehemiah was done with the surprise attacks on his people. He had had enough! He began stationing people all around the wall to keep watch day and night. No longer would their enemy attack them without their knowledge. If the enemy was coming, they would be ready for them!

Reflect and Respond

In our verse today, we see that Nehemiah's enemies were planning a surprise attack. However, Nehemiah became aware of their schemes and was able to make a plan of his own, allowing the Israelites to defended themselves against their enemy. Obviously it is extremely important that we recognize the enemy will attack; it doesn't have to be a surprise! We can be prepared and have a plan.

Fight

How can the knowledge of knowing you are in a battle with a real opponent help you become stronger?

What preparations can you make to arm yourself for the battle ahead?

What feelings do these words evoke within you?

Enemy	Fight	Unaware
Battle	Defend	Unprepared

Build

Our sin nature causes all of us to fail at times, and often it is difficult to recognize just how Satan plays a role in those situations. As obstacles and trials enter your life, ask God to show you if there is a bigger war being waged. Journal about an area of your life where Satan may be trying to attack. Pray for God's strength and guidance in this situation.

Day Three

Living on the Extremes

Today's scripture reading: Nehemiah 6:2

Have you ever woken up from a slumber to realize you were in the middle of a war you somehow seemed to be completely unaware of until that moment? Life was hard, and things kept coming up that took you two steps back each time you took one step forward, but you blew it off as life. Then the fog lifted, and you realized it wasn't just normal life—it was an attack on you, your testimony, and your family.

A few years ago, Wade, my husband, went back to school for another four-year degree. (Yes, I said *another*, but that's a different story.) To say it was a really hard time for us would be an understatement. Yet I thought it was a season that we would have to push through as part of "normal" life.

We seldom saw each other.

When he was home, I knew it was important for our three children to spend time with him. He would spend a few moments with them, help me tuck them in bed, and then head out again to study. Our communication and time together went out the door. Yet before the door swung shut, in walked a familiar friend named Anger. I was angry at him for not balancing it all, upset he wasn't making me a priority, and angry I was left doing everything on my own.

As I got acquainted with Anger, Resentment settled in, and I built a wall that pushed my hard-working husband out instead of building a wall of safety and protection around our marriage.

One day, after months of pent-up emotions, I cried out to the Lord. You know the kind, where it looks more like a temper tantrum a three-year-old would have? Yep, that was me! I cried and yelled and told God my honest feelings, knowing my Father would listen without judgment and see through to my true heart's cry.

Then in the middle of my ranting and raving, God whispered His truth quietly in my spirit. "You're fighting a battle, love. Do you want to win, or do you want to lose?"

"A battle? What are you talking about, God? I'm just mad—spitting mad, if you can't tell!"

"No, sweet daughter, you are not. You are allowing Satan to gain a foothold in your marriage because of the way *you* are acting. If you don't want to lose this fight against Satan, you had better let Me fight for you and with you!"

I had no clue I was fighting a battle. I knew I had an enemy; we talked about it in church every once in a while. But amid my normal life? No. I never really thought about Satan attacking me personally. Plus, I always thought, *If I don't think about him, maybe he will leave me alone!*

It wasn't until the Lord lifted the fog of unawareness that I realized the truth. I was in a battle, and I had better pick up my sword and start fighting!

Life is full of ups and downs. Not every difficult situation we go through is an attack from Satan. Let me repeat: not everything bad we go through is from Satan! But we can't pretend that he isn't real. Living unaware of our enemy allows him to gain ground in our lives. We also don't need to be afraid of him. We are on the winning side, my friend!

Living on either extreme is dangerous—hypersensitive to Satan and his schemes, or unaware with no thought of Satan.

On one hand, if we live on the extreme side of being hypersensitive to Satan, everything in our life becomes his fault. People living from this viewpoint tend to blame Satan for almost everything, leaving no room for sin or consequences to their own choices in life. "The devil made me do it," they say. They are thinking about Satan and his schemes more than God and His Word. That is a dangerous place to be!

On the other hand, if we live unaware with no thought or regard to Satan at all, it's almost like he doesn't exist. We are knocked off our feet every time something bad happens in life, fall prey to temptation easily, and think life should be all roses. This is also a dangerous place to be!

We need to become aware of Satan in our lives and the world around us. We should acknowledge him for who he is—not giving him unjust time and attention, but having awareness so we can stand up and fight when God calls us to do so.

Reflect and Respond

The Bible is clear. We have an enemy who is real and wants to deceive us. But many times we are fighting the wrong battle. Satan deceives us into thinking everyone else is the bad guy!

Read Ephesians 6:12 (NIV) below. Who does God tell us our real enemy is?

> For our struggle is not against flesh and blood, but against the rulers, against the authorities, against the powers of this dark world and against the spiritual forces of evil in the heavenly realms.

Maybe you are like me and need to be reminded that your struggle is not against flesh and blood. Your struggle goes much deeper, and once you realize this, the fog will begin to lift and you will be able to fight the real battle!

Fight

Has there been a time you woke up to the awareness that Satan was medaling in your life?

Is there a struggle you're going through right now that could be more than just "normal life"?

Build

What is one action step God is asking you to take in response to this awareness?

What does living on the extremes look like?

When it comes to living on the extremes, where would you rate yourself?

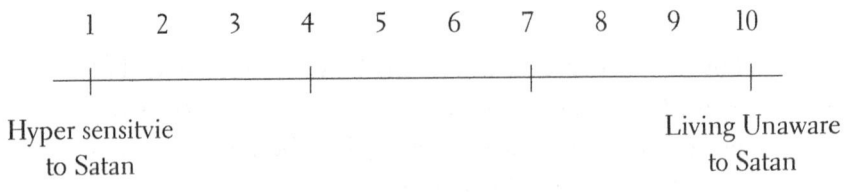

1   2   3   4   5   6   7   8   9   10

Hyper sensitvie   Living Unaware
to Satan   to Satan

Why is it important to live with a balanced view instead of living on either end?

Take some time to journal a prayer to God about a struggle with which you have been dealing. Ask him to show you any area in which Satan has been attacking you personally.

Day Four
Strategic Planning

Today's scripture reading: Proverbs 16:3 (NIV)

Wade and I are "do-it-yourselfers." Not only does it save us money, but there is a sense of accomplishment along the way (although the money is the main reason!). Yet sometimes when we start one of these home projects, it ends with an argument. He has his way of doing something, I have my way, and the two don't line up! In the end, we walk away wondering why we didn't pay someone to do it for us in the first place. Anyone else feel my pain?

As we approached our next project of remodeling the kitchen, I felt the Holy Spirit tugging at my heart and telling me to act different this time around. Yet in order for me to react out of His empowerment and not my own, I needed to get prepared. Knowing where I was likely to get upset, lose my temper, or pull away in stubbornness (the areas I needed to change) was key in helping me decide how to act differently this time around. How do I typically react, and how does God want me to react? I needed His help and gentle voice guiding me along the way. I needed a plan!

Demo day arrived, and our big project began.

There was so much work to be done and so many decisions to be made, but God's gentle spirit was guiding me. I reacted differently. I spoke with love and patience, and I worked hard with a good spirit. Don't get me wrong; I didn't get it right 100 percent of the time, but in the end we completed the biggest project we had ever started together; instead of arguing over piddly things, we walked away proud of what we had accomplished!

I prepared for the battle I knew would come by making a plan and choosing *beforehand* to react as God would have me react instead of the way I wanted to.

Preparing for Battle

Meanwhile, the people in Judah said, "The strength of the laborers is giving out, and there is so much rubble that we cannot rebuild the wall." Also our enemies said, "Before they know it or see us, we will be right there among them and will kill them and put an end to the work." Then the Jews who lived near them came and told us ten times over, "Wherever you turn, they will attack us." Therefore I stationed some of the people behind the lowest points of the wall at the exposed places, posting them by families, with their swords, spears and bows. After I looked things over, I stood up and said to the nobles, the officials and the rest of the people, "Don't be afraid of them. Remember the Lord, who is great and awesome, and fight for your families, your sons and your daughters, your wives and your homes." … From that day on, half of my men did the work, while the other half were equipped with spears, shields, bows and armor. The officers posted themselves behind all the people of Judah, who were building the wall. Those who carried materials did their work with one hand and held a weapon in the other, and each of the builders wore his sword at his side as he worked. (Nehemiah 4:10–18 NIV)

The Israelites were on the verge of quitting. They were tired, stressed, and in fear for their lives. Anytime the Israelites stepped out in faith to obey God's call, fear was one step behind. Many times their fear prevented them from completing the task.

But this time was going to be different.

The Israelites realized their enemy had plans to attack them. Nehemiah, with resolve and no quit in him, made a plan of his own. He stationed people behind the gaps in their walls, the places they knew their enemy would attack first. The gaps were the vulnerable areas known by their enemy. Defending the exposed areas became their number one priority.

Nehemiah took their typical response of fear and moved them to action. They didn't just sit there—they moved. In the past, fear had stopped them from continuing what God had called them to do. But this time, the Israelites began to sharpen their sword by making a plan to help them defend against their enemy.

They acknowledged their vulnerable areas and began preparing for the attack. The Israelites were able to defend against their enemies by stationing people in the weak areas first, by keeping watch day and night, and by never letting down their guard. Victory was theirs as they completed the task that God called them to do!

Reflect and Respond

Knowing your weakest areas of life, where you are most vulnerable, will allow you to predict where an attack might come first.

Even though it is hard to sit a think of our own weak and vulnerabilities, it is imperative if we want to live the empowered life God has called us to. It is in our weakness that Christ can become our strength that we bend low and admit we can't do it without Him, that we relinquish control and allow Him to take over. Because where we are weak, He is strong!

> That is why, for Christ's sake, I delight in weaknesses,
> in insults, in hardships, in persecutions, in difficulties.
> For when I am weak, then I am strong. (2 Corinthians
> 12:10 NIV)

Fight

Take a few minutes to think about where your weak areas might be. Is there a trend in your life, like I saw in mine, where you act contrary to how God wants you to act?

How could these be weak areas in someone's life?

- Busy lifestyle
- Anger
- Sharp tongue
- Bad attitude
- Vanity
- Caring about other people's opinions
- Always saying yes
- A little unorganized
- A little overorganized
- Opinionated
- Shy

Build

Taking a weak area you identify with above, write out a new plan of action that will change how you respond in the future.

How I typically react: How God wants me to react:

Change doesn't happen overnight, and it defiantly won't happen without a plan. Little by little, if we pick up our swords and fight against it, God can give us victory!

Day Five

Discouragement Turned Determination

Today's scripture reading: Isaiah 41:10 (NLV)

Being a mom is the hardest thing I have ever done! It takes me to all extremes, from the happiest I have ever been to the saddest, from the most joyous to the angriest, from full of energy and life to exhausted and at my wits end, and everything in between. It challenges me to be better, do better, laugh more, slow down more, play more. Hands down, motherhood is the hardest calling God has ever given me.

There have been countless times I have felt completely alone and misunderstood. Then there are times I seem to be my worst critic, beating myself up for days long after the apology and forgiveness was given. I have had long nights lying in bed, thinking of all the things I could have done or should have done, and making a resolution to do better tomorrow, only to fail first thing in the morning because I didn't get enough sleep!

Discouragement from others has caught me off guard as well. There are seemingly innocent questions: "How will you manage your busy schedule? Is this the best timing for your family? Who will help you? Who will fund your ministry? And on and on. No doubt they are putting voices to thoughts and fears with which I have already wrestled God. Yet as their voices echo in my soul, reluctance grows as I begin to doubt all over again, crashing into a brick wall of discouragement.

Discouragement stops us in our tracks, speaking lies to us, causing hesitation and doubt, and we are unable to accomplish what God has commissioned. If the enemy stops us, then others will never see the victory God can bring in our lives. Worse yet, if we allow discouragement to hold us down, we will never live the empowered lives we were meant for!

Satan tends to use the same schemes over and over again in my life and in your life. Do you know why? Because they work! It's time to wise up, girls! We can fight back and stop him dead in his tracks!

Discouragement

Look for how discouragement is used in these verses.

> When Sanballat heard that we were rebuilding the wall, he became angry and was greatly incensed. He ridiculed the Jews, and in the presence of his associates and the army of Samaria, he said, "What are those feeble Jews doing? Will they restore their wall? Will they offer sacrifices? Will they finish in a day? Can they bring the stones back to life from those heaps of rubble—burned as they are?"
>
> Tobiah the Ammonite, who was at his side, said, "What they are building—even a fox climbing up on it would break down their wall of stones!" (Nehemiah 4:1–3 NIV)

Once they began building what God had called them to, the Israelites were ridiculed and mocked by outsiders. Sanballat and Tobiah mocked them in front of other people, to their faces, and behind their backs. Can you relate?

Their enemies did not wait to ridicule and discourage them. They didn't let them get comfortable with their new jobs or be confident in what God called them to do. No, the enemy came in full force from the *beginning*, even before the building began.

But what did Nehemiah and the Israelites do?

As discouragement was beginning to set in, Nehemiah prayed. He prayed to his God—not a foreign or distant god, not a god who sits idly by and judges every motive, but a God who loves His people and empowers them to accomplish more than they ever dreamed possible.

After Sanballat and Tobiah discouraged the Israelites, we read these victorious words: "So we rebuilt the wall till all of it reached half its height, for the people worked with all their heart" (Nehemiah 4:6 NIV).

Instead of letting discouragement stop them from their work, they used it to bring resolve and renewed commitment to their calling. God turned their discouragement into determination when they remembered who He was. Not who they were or their own capabilities, but who their God was and what He was capable of! "Don't be afraid of them. Remember the great and awe-inspiring Lord" (Nehemiah 4:14 NIV).

Many times when we get discouraged, we start thinking of our own limitations and our lack of abilities. If we would stop and meditate on God, we would remember from whom our strength comes. We serve an empowering God! He doesn't leave us to fend for ourselves but walks beside us each step of the way.

> Don't be afraid, for I am with you. Don't be discouraged, for I am your God. I will strengthen you and help you. I will hold you up with my victorious right hand. (Isaiah 41:10 NLV)

God is with you, and therefore you don't need to be discouraged! Stop listening to the unwanted taunts of others. Yahweh is your God! This verse gives us hope as it reminds us God is our strength and help. His powerful and almighty right hand will hold us up when we have no strength and when our legs give way under the pressure of others disbelief. He, my friend, will carry us through! For when we are weak, He is strong (2 Corinthians 12:9–11 NIV).

Reflect and Respond

Satan will use discouragement to try to stop us from accomplishing what God has called us to, but God can turn discouragement into determination when we remember who He is!

Do you recall a time when God took your discouragement and turned it into determination, igniting a fire deep within as you were propelled from your state of idleness to a full-out sprint to win the battle?

Fight

Is there any evidence of discouragement in your life right now? Is it stopping you from accomplishing what God has called you to do?

Take some time to remember who God is to you. What has He done for you in the past? How has He shown love to you lately? How has He protected you in the past and present? God's Word says He is the same yesterday, today, and forevermore. (Hebrews 13:8 NIV).

Build

One of the ways I combat discouragement in my life is through scripture memory. Write a verse or two on a note card and post it somewhere you will see it throughout the day. Choose a verse that encourages you and reminds you of God's power in your life so He can speak truth into your heart. Here are a few to get you started.

> Cast your cares on the LORD and he will sustain you;
> he will never let the righteous be shaken. (Psalm 55:22 NIV)

The Lord himself goes before you and will be with you; he will never leave you nor forsake you. Do not be afraid; do not be discouraged. (2 Chronicles 32:7 NIV)

The righteous cry out, and the LORD hears them; he delivers them from all their troubles. The LORD is close to the brokenhearted and saves those who are crushed in spirit. (Psalm 34:17–18 NIV)

The Lord himself goes before you and will be with you; he will never leave you nor forsake you. Do not be afraid; do not be discouraged. (Deuteronomy 31:8 NIV)

Day Six

Beyond the Distractions of Life

Nothing is more frustrating to me than starting my day with a long list of to-dos, a blank calendar to get things done, and an attitude in which to accomplish them, only to find myself at the end of the day without anything on my list done! What happened? Where did my day go?

Short answer: distractions!

Getting distracted happens to all of us, and no matter how hard we try, there will be days nothing on the to-do list gets checked off. There will always be more pressing issues that arise and take over our day.

Overwhelmed and distracted—that's right where Satan wants the people of God. We have so many things to do that asking God what He wants us to accomplish isn't an issue at all. Pausing for prayer would take up too much valuable time! Listening and talking to God seems to be the last thing on everyone's to-do list. Busy, busy, busy! Maybe one of our biggest failures when it comes to fighting against Satan is- distractions!

Could distractions really be a scheme of Satan, or is it simply a natural consequence of being too busy and unorganized?

Let's take a look at Nehemiah 6:1–3 (NIV) and see if we can gain some insight.

It was told to Sanballat, Tobiah, Geshem the Arab, and to the rest of those who hated us that I had built the wall again. They were told that the wall had no more open places, but I had not yet set up the doors in the gates. So Sanballat and Geshem sent word to me, saying, "Come, let us meet together in one of the villages in the plain of Ono." But they were planning to hurt or kill me. So I sent men with word to them, saying, "I am doing a great work and I cannot come down. Why should the work stop while I leave it and come down to you?" They sent word to me four times in this way, and I gave them the same answer.

Because discouragement wasn't working to stop the building of the wall, Sanballat, Tobiah, and Geshem needed another strategy. Distraction became their new plan of attack, and this time it was against Nehemiah. If they could get Nehemiah, the leader of the Israelite people, to falter, then they could get the whole community to fall!

On outward appearances, it looked as if Sanballat and the others were inviting Nehemiah to join them for a friendly conversation, maybe one of reconciliation or a time of rest from hard work.

However, Nehemiah saw through their scheme, and instead of looking at outward appearances, he saw their true motives. Nehemiah, using discernment, recognized the true intention of his enemies was to harm him and bring destruction upon his people.

According to the theologian David Guzik, "Discernment is the ability to judge matters according to God's view of them, and not according to their outward appearance" (https://www.blueletterbible.org/Comm/ guzik_david/StudyGuide2017-Neh/Neh-6.cfm?a=419003).

Outward appearances can be so deceiving. Yet someone with discernment can pause, look beyond outward appearances, and see the consequences of a choice before it happens. Biblical discernment doesn't stop at knowledge, though. We must move beyond just knowing.

the good and righteous choice to *obeying* what God calls us to do. True biblical discernment moves us toward obedience.

Nehemiah questions the long-term effects Sanballat's proposal had on him. "I am doing a great work and I cannot come down. Why should the work stop while I leave it and come down to you?" Nehemiah 6:3 (NIV).

Not only did Nehemiah use discernment to understand the real motives of his enemies, but he also knew the work would cease and falter if he left. That was a risk he was not willing to take. Five times his enemies beckoned him to come, and five times he resisted their distraction. Nehemiah's discernment lead to a focus that was steadfast and unwavering. He was unwavering in accomplish what God called him to do. He put all distractions aside, buckled down, and did the work God called him to do.

After Sanballat attempted to distract Nehemiah, he responded, "But now my God strengthen me" (Nehemiah 6:9b HCSB). Another interpretation is "So now I increase my efforts" (HCSB study Bible notes, 783). We see how discernment led Nehemiah to a renewed determination.

Every time the enemy tried to discourage Nehemiah, he increased his efforts. Through the strength of God, Nehemiah was able to continue in his calling with renewed effort.

Reflect and Respond

With God's help, you will begin to turn your distractions into discernment and determination to accomplish the calling God has for you. Allow God to reignite focus in your life when distractions come your way by looking beyond the outward appearances and seeing things through God's perspective.

Fight

What is your biggest distraction in accomplishing your calling?

What long-term consequences could you face if you continue to follow that distraction?

Build

What can these verses teach us about gaining discernment?

> Who is wise? Let them *realize* these things. Who is discerning? Let them *understand*. The ways of the LORD are right; the righteous *walk* in them, but the rebellious stumble in them. (Hosea 14:9 NIV)

Write the three italicized words from the verse above.

_____

_____

_____

What do these three words help us understand about discernment?

If any of you lacks wisdom, you should ask God, who gives generously to all without finding fault, and it will be given to you. (James 1:5 NIV)

But solid food is for the mature, for those who have their powers of discernment trained by constant practice to distinguish good from evil. (Hebrews 5:14 ESV)

Day Seven

Disillusionment to Revealed Deception

Today's scripture reading: Nehemiah 6:11

While on vacation, my husband and I thought it would be fun to visit a church in a new area. We walked in to friendly greetings and warm handshakes. The music was wonderful; the band was full of energy and talent. The people were kind, thoughtful, and full of life. Everyone seemed to enjoy being there. As the pastor approached the pulpit to speak, we sat hopeful with pens in hand, ready to take notes so we wouldn't forget the wisdom he was about to impart. The more the pastor talked, the more we enjoyed the message, yet we wrote nothing. We leaned in closer to hear every word. Surely there was something worth writing down!

And then his words become clanging cymbals in our ears as he began to speak boastfully about a man he mentored, a popular TV evangelist we regarded as a false teacher.

The minute his words didn't line up with the truth of God's Word was the minute we stopped listening. Upon recognizing the deception, we left heartbroken for all who were deceived, taking this man's words over God's Word.

Deception from the Beginning

"In the beginning God created the heavens and the earth and everything in them" (Genesis 1:1 NIV). The centerpiece of God's creation was the Garden of Eden. Within the garden, He placed his prize creation, Adam and Eve. Their job was to care for the garden and all the creatures that lived there. One day, a serpent came to them and began talking.

> He said to the woman, "Did God say that you should not eat from any tree in the garden?" Then the woman said to the snake, "We may eat the fruit of the trees of the garden. But from the tree which is in the center of the garden, God has said, 'Do not eat from it or touch it, or you will die.'" The snake said to the woman, "No, you for sure will not die! For God knows that when you eat from it, your eyes will be opened and you will be like God, knowing good and bad." The woman saw that the tree was good for food, and pleasing to the eyes, and could fill the desire of making one wise. So she took of its fruit and ate. She also gave some to her husband, and he ate. Then the eyes of both of them were opened, and they knew they were without clothes. So they sewed fig leaves together and made themselves clothing. (Genesis 3:1–7 NIV)

We see that from the very beginning, Satan questioning Eve's beliefs about God. His question brought doubt into her mind. As doubt crept in, sin appeared more and more enticing, causing Eve to think there may be another truth other than God's.

He disillusioned her with his deceitfulness, and Eve took the bait, eating the forbidden fruit. It worked! He won!

According to Dictionary.com, the definition of disillusion is:

1. to free from or deprive of illusion, belief, idealism, etc.; disenchant
2. a freeing or a being freed from illusion or conviction; disenchantment

The definition of distraction is "to free from illusion or belief."

Satan disguises himself as truth. He wraps up temptation and sin in a warm, fuzzy blanket, enticing us to relax on the couch of luxury. However, he never reveals the truth of sin—how it ruins lives, destroys families, and leaves people alone and miserable. He begins with questions about God's real love and goodness. Then, when we begin to hesitate in our belief, Satan flashes an enticing invitation, wrapped as truth, to make us turn away from God. We take the bait just like Eve.

Using a man posing as a prophet named Shemiah, Nehemiah's enemies attempt to disillusion him as well. Shemaiah urged Nehemiah to enter into the sacred area of the temple to avoid attempts by his enemies to assassinate him, insinuating that God would surely spare him. As the prophet instructed him to disobey God's law (Numbers 18:7), Nehemiah responded.

> Why would a man like me run for cover? And why would a man like me use The Temple as a hideout? I won't do it.
>
> I sensed that God hadn't sent this man. The so-called prophecy he spoke to me was the work of Tobiah and Sanballat; they had hired him. He had been hired to scare me off—trick me—a layman, into desecrating The Temple and ruining my good reputation so they could accuse me. (Nehemiah 6:11–13 NIV)

Just as he did with discouragement and distraction, Nehemiah recognized disillusionment from his enemies. He instantly knew that the "truth" Shemaiah was speaking was false because it went directly against God's word.

The truth of God's Word pierced through the lies of his oppressors like a double-edged sword. Nehemiah recognized the trap and turned away from listening to Shamaiah to avoid the trap.

Reflect and Respond

Just like Nehemiah, we must know what God's Word says so when anyone speaks against it, we will recognize it as deception.

When you sense something odd about a thought you have, a word someone speaks, or a situation you find yourself in, stop and take heed. Step back and hold it up against the truth of God's Word. Does it align? Does it have consistent truth, or does it fall flat? Allow God's Word to turn the disillusionment of Satan into revealed deception.

Fight

How has Satan disillusioned you before? Is there anything you believe right now that doesn't line up with what God's Word says?

Sometimes we don't even think about what we believe. We simply believe it out of habit, or we grew up with certain beliefs that aren't necessarily God's beliefs. Second Corinthians 10:5 (HCSB) tells us to "take every thought captive.". Maybe there are some things you need to bring before the Lord, allowing Him to show you the deception in what you have been thinking and maybe even teaching to your family.

Write down one or two situations where you have wondered what God would say about that issue.

Build

Seek the Bible for your one or two situations above Ask a pastor, Sunday school teacher, or mentor what they believe God teaches on those issues.

We demolish arguments and every pretension that sets itself up against the knowledge of God, and we take captive every thought to make it obedient to Christ. (2 Corinthians 10:5 NIV)

Commit to taking hold of your thoughts, bringing them under the conviction of God's Word.

God has given you the weapon against disillusionment, the Holy Bible. Study it, memorize it, read it, and preach it! As His word grows within your heart and mind, you will recognize more and more the discouragement, distractions, and the disillusions of Satan.

Make a commitment to read God's Word daily.

Conclusion

Part of Satan's motive (to destroy all that God has called us to do and be) involves those people who shadow our every move. No matter how old or young we are, we have people who are following our lead. Satan knows the effect his schemes can have on our lives. He also recognizes those around us who witness how we act, live, worship, spend our money, and so forth. Just like in Nehemiah, if Satan can take down the leader, then he knows he can take down the whole community.

One of my favorite verses in Nehemiah is, "Don't be afraid of them. Remember the great and awe-inspiring Lord, and fight for your countrymen, your sons and daughters, your wives and homes" (Nehemiah 4:14 NIV).

Sometimes as women, it's hard to pick up the sword and fight for ourselves. For countless reasons, we put others first, attending to the needs of others before our own and even before the calling God has commissioned us to.

But stir within us a need to fight for someone else—our friends, our sons, our daughters, or our husbands? Well, game on, sister! Mama bear is about to roar! It is innate in us to fight for those we love, isn't it?

Let us not be deceived, though. When Satan attacks you, defeats you, and pulls you down, he pulls down all those you love as well. We must stand up and fight against our enemy in our own lives first!

We must do the following.

- Recognize we are in a fight
- Walk in obedience despite the opposition
- Stop living the extreme beliefs about Satan

- Make a plan by knowing our weak areas
- Recognize discouragement and allow God to turn it into determination
- Recognize distraction and ask God for discernment
- Recognize disillusion and seek God's revealed deception

When we begin fighting back our enemy in our own personal lives, we are fighting for our countrymen, sons and daughters, spouses, and homes. We are fighting for them by teaching them, through our example, how to defeat Satan and his schemes in their lives too.

If you want to build something for God, by all means pick up that hammer, but don't forget your sword! The minute you declare victory for God is the minute you declare war against Satan.

But remember, "Don't be afraid of them. Remember the great and awe-inspiring Lord, and fight for your countrymen, your sons and daughters, your wives and homes" (Nehemiah 4:14 NIV).

Why do we fight? Because of our great God and for all those who follow behind!

Week Four

Leaving a Legacy by

Day One

Becoming a Keeper of the Faith

Today's scripture reading: Nehemiah 2:17; Nehemiah 7:1–3

I am a keeper of the Box. For thirty-three years, it has been in the top of my closet. It's a plain old cardboard box. There is nothing special about the box, but it's what is stored on the inside that is priceless to me. You see, it holds all that I own of my son, Daniel Keith, whom we lost at birth. The first thing I see upon opening the box is a multicolored pastel crocheted blanket lovingly made by a dear, sweet, church member. Toward the bottom of the box is a heart-shaped white frame with the only photo I have of my sweet boy. Tucked inside among a few other items are the cards and letters from friends and family, with handwritten notes of love and affection.

As you can imagine, in the years right after Daniel's death, this box came down from the top of my closet on a regular basis. It was helpful in my healing as God began rebuilding that area of my heart. Now, after many years, the box doesn't come down all that often. However, there are still occasions when I get the box down, reach in, and pull out those tear-stained and rumpled journal pages—pages on which I had poured out my grief and recorded my prayers along with scripture that, during those painful days, had begun the process of healing my heart. I will then take those notes of yesterday, make copies, and slip them into an envelope to mail to another brokenhearted mother, adding a note that reads, "I, too, lost a child like you!" As I send it off with a prayer, I ask the Lord to allow this broken area of my life, which has been rebuilt through His empowerment, to in some way help bring healing to another.

As mothers, grandmothers, wives, and career women, we are responsible for the keeping of many things. We are not just keepers of the gum, the score, the secrets, the family albums, or even the wedding dresses still hanging in our closets. We are keepers of what matters most: we are keepers of our faith.

God was talking with Moses and said, "Say this to the Israelites: Yahweh, the God of your fathers, the God of Abraham, the God of Isaac, and the God of Jacob, has sent me to you. This is My name forever; this is how I am to be remembered in every generation" (Exodus 3:15 HCSB).

God desires His name be passed down to every generation by those who are keepers of His faith.

As Christian women, it is our responsibility to possess an authentic relationship with Yahweh, the one true God. As keepers of that truth, we are to understand the importance of what we keep and pass it to the next generation. We live in a world where the walls of Christianity are in ruin, and God's name has fallen in disgrace because of our generation has compromised by living in disobedience. The future faith of those we love is in jeopardy. We must tell the stories of what our God has done for us, so His name can be remembered in every generation.

In Nehemiah 7:1 (HCSB), we read that Nehemiah appointed three positions of great importance. These positions helped him accomplish the great task of being the keeper of his faith and restoring the nation of Israel back to their God: "When the wall had been rebuilt and I had the doors installed, the gatekeepers, singers, and Levites were appointed." During our time together, we will discover how the gatekeepers, singers, and Levites can spur us forward in becoming keepers of the faith and in leaving a godly legacy to the next generation by keeping God's vision, keeping God's praise, and keeping God's truth. If we accept this challenge, we too can live a life worth remembering and leave a godly legacy like Abraham, Isaac, Jacob, and Nehemiah.

An important part of being a keeper is knowing that you are not the keeper of the things God has entrusted to you for your sole benefit. They are also for the benefit of those who are coming behind.

Reflect and Respond

What is in your box? You have situations in your life through which God has brought you. In that process, He has redefined who He is to you. Perhaps He has revealed Himself to you as your provider, your protector, or your counselor. It is my prayer you have also found Him to be the Savior because He brought you out of the bondage of sin. As the keeper of these stories, your responsibility is to reveal who God is by sharing your stories with those with whom you live side by side and with those who are coming behind.

Fight

Write in your journal at least one experience through which God brought you and how you could help others in a similar situation. Record the life lessons you learned as God rebuilt that area of your life and how He revealed Himself to you.

Build

Plan a way you can take that experience and share it with someone to begin passing your faith on to others (e.g., phone call, letter, or personal visit). Journal your action plan and the responses you receive.

Day Two

The Gatekeepers

The Great Wall of China took hundreds of years to build, but it was necessary to protect China against attacks from the north. A survey found that the entire wall, with all its branches, measures out to 13,171 miles. It is said that as many as four hundred thousand people died during the wall's construction. It is one of the few human-made objects astronauts can see from outer space as they look back at Earth. Despite all the effort and sacrifices and its massive size, the wall was unsuccessful in keeping out the enemy. Do you know why? All the enemy had to do to enter was bribe a gatekeeper. The enemy on the inside, let in the enemy on the outside.

Second Chronicles 23:19 (HCSB) states, "He stationed gatekeepers at the gates of the LORD's temple so that nothing unclean could enter for any reason." It is a huge responsibility to be appointed the position of gatekeeper. The gatekeeper's responsibility is to say no to the forces that bring evil into the city. Gatekeepers were the first line of defense in protecting the people from turning away from their God, but the walls of Jerusalem had crumbled because Israel had allowed the sin of idolatry to walk right through the gate. God had warned His people to not intermarry with the pagan nations because it would bring pagan worship into the city. However, His people did not listen and allowed their sons and daughters to marry and have families with those who did not believe in the one true God. This resulted in idol worship entering their culture, and it began the erosion of their faith in Yahweh. Nehemiah knew there could be no compromise with evil if the city was to be restored back to the one true God.

The men who were appointed to the position of gatekeeper were important because they determined the spiritual direction of the city. Nehemiah 7:2 (HCSB) says, "Then I put my brother Hanani in charge of Jerusalem, along with Hananiah, commander of the fortress, because he was a faithful man who feared God more than most." How does a gatekeeper remain faithful? By fearing the Lord! Throughout scripture, we are exhorted to fear the Lord.

Don't be confused and think you should be afraid of God. To fear God means to have a deep respect for Him and reverence for His commands; it means to take God seriously. Proverbs 8:13 (HCSB) says, "To fear the LORD is to hate evil." God tell us to hate evil because He hates evil. God knows that when evil enters the life of believers, it corrupts and destroys the relationship we have with Him. We must do everything we can to remove evil from our lives and from the lives of those whom we have been entrusted to guard.

We are tasked with the responsibility of guarding the entrances to the hearts of those who are entrusted to our care. With computers, video games, televisions, and cellular phones, there are more entrances to the heart than ever before. We are called to be the gatekeepers standing between our entrusted and the world, protecting them from the enemy. It is impossible to do this if we allow the enemy access to our own hearts and lives. God's vision for us is that we will remain faithful to Him.

Just as Nehemiah was commissioned to bring the people back to a relationship with Jehovah, we too are commissioned to remain faithful and obedient to bring others to a saving knowledge of the Lord. God wants us to be like Him and think like Him; He wants us to hate evil as He hates evil. "To fear the Lord" means we will be faithful gatekeepers, serious in doing all we can to remove evil from our lives and from the lives of those we love. A woman who fears the Lord will leave a godly legacy by being diligent to guard her gates, not only keeping out sin but keeping her own heart pure.

Reflect and Respond

The gatekeeper teaches us to be keepers of God's vision. The gatekeeper's responsibility in Nehemiah's day was to restore the people back to a faithful relationship with the one true God. As today's gatekeepers, we are to keep that same vision by not only helping others return to God but also remaining faithful to Him as our only true God.

Fight

Our world is constantly enticing us to blatantly abandon the truth that there is only one God and only one way to God, through Jesus Christ. In what area of your life is your battle greatest in keeping God first?

Build

William Cowper, the noted eighteenth-century poet and hymnist, said, "Satan trembles when he sees the weakest saint upon their knees."[4] So, put up your guard! What comes to mind as the place to start in putting God first today?

---

[4] Adrian Rogers, Ten Secrets for a Successful Family (Wheaton, IL: Crossway Books, 1996), 116.
https://www.gotquestions.org/fear-God.html. "William Cowper Quotes," Brainy Quote, 2017, https://www.brainyquote.com/quotes/authors/w/william_cowper.html.

What one action can you do that will resist sin and strengthen God as your priority?

Start implementing this step today.

Day Three

Jubilant Praise

Today's scripture reading: Colossians 3:16; Chronicles 9:33

When I was young, for many years I woke to the sounds of gospel music. Every Sunday morning, my mother would turn the television to *The Gospel Singing Jubilee*. It became known as the longest running television program in the history of gospel music. Many of you who are my age may remember waking to the musical strains of, "Jubilee, jubilee ... you're invited to this happy jubilee!" My mother loved the Florida Boys, the Happy Goodman Family, and Dixie Echoes as they sang those old-time gospel songs. Me, not so much. I would cringe as that music echoed through my room and woke me on those early Sunday mornings. Little did I know that those verses and tunes would forever be part of my spiritual heritage.

The second position that Nehemiah appointed was that of the singers, who represent being keepers of God's praise. Their responsibility was to keep God's praise always before the people. First Chronicles 9:33 says that the singers were on duty all day and all night. Second Chronicles 5:13 (HCSB) states, "The trumpeters and singers joined together to praise and thank the LORD with one voice. They raised their voices, accompanied by trumpets, cymbals, and musical instruments, in praise to the LORD: For He is good; His faithful love endures forever." There was singing in the Lord's house twenty-four hours a day! This position was so important that Nehemiah records over two hundred singers assigned to the city of God. He wanted God's city to continually be filled with God's praise.

Remember, Nehemiah's mission was to bring the people back to a personal relationship with their God. His main goal was to return the

Israelites in the city of Jerusalem back to being God's holy people so they could be a testimony for the glory of God once again. He wasn't just bringing them back to survive—he wanted them to flourish in the land. To do this, they needed a genuine relationship with God.

Our family is large! It's our joke that we do everything in herds. With four daughters, four sons-in-law, and eleven grandchildren, we make up a big crew! When my first granddaughter was two, she was trying to learn who we all were. One evening as her mother was putting her to bed, she began to cry. When my daughter asked her what was wrong, she said, "I want my people!" She didn't want to go to bed; she wanted to be with all her family!

God feels the same way: He desires a relationship with all His people! One of the most repeated phrases of the Bible is found in Exodus 6:7 (HCSB): "I will take you as My people, and I will be your God. You will know that I am Yahweh your God, who delivered you from the forced labor of the Egyptians." Look at it again in the New Testament in Hebrews 8:10 (HCSB): "But this is the covenant that I will make with the house of Israel after those days, says the Lord: I will put My laws into their minds and write them on their hearts. I will be their God, and they will be My people." Repeatedly in scripture, God says that He wants us to be His people, and He will be our God. This brings me chills knowing that the God of the universe wants to be my personal God and wants me to be part of His people! As a singer of His praise, we have the privilege to express to others our love and devotion for our God.

Reflect and Respond

When we praise God, we are elevating one's opinion of Him by giving Him honor and praise for what He has done. Praising God is simply giving Him the recognition He deserves. We give glory and praise to our God with the use of our physical bodies (singing, clapping, dancing), with our hearts and minds (praying, studying His Word, meditating on and memorizing scripture), and with our deeds (proclaiming to others what He has done for us)—the list is endless. In all our methods of praising God, the result must be that God is elevated to the highest position of worship, and it should create within ourselves and others a sense of awe and wonder of God's power, love, and grace.

Fight

We have the same mission as Nehemiah: to live a life that brings honor and glory to God. Unlike Nehemiah, we won't find ourselves building a stone wall around a city, but as godly wives, moms, employees, teachers, and all the roles in which we find ourselves, we must be faithful to bring praise continually into our hearts, homes, communities, churches, and everywhere we go. How is your life expressing praise to God and bringing Him honor?

Build

Read the verses below that proclaim God's desire to be your God. Write a prayer of praise to Him, thanking Him for being your God.

- Leviticus 26:12
- Jeremiah 7:23; 24:7; 30:22
- Ezekiel 11:20; 14:11; 37:23; 37:27
- Hosea 2:23
- Zechariah 8:8
- 2 Corinthians 6:16
- Revelation 21:1–3

Day Four

Model of Praise

"Could you just sit still and behave?" were the words out of my mouth as I hurriedly tried to get ready to leave the house for women's Bible study one morning. However, with three small daughters dancing around my feet, it was becoming obvious that I was going to be late. Finally, out of frustration I took Amy, my youngest daughter at the time; placed her on the vanity; and told her she would have to sit still until I was ready. She squirmed and wiggled and attempted to get into my makeup, which brought more rebuke on my part. Excitedly, she asked in her sweet little voice, "Well, can I at least sing a song?" My reply was something to the extent, "Of course you can sing, if you just sit still!" To that, she began to sing, "I'm so glad my mommy loves Jesus, so she won't be cranky!"

Ouch! Here I was trying to leave to go study the Word of God, and my witness to my children was anything but an example of Christ. Yet my sweet little child gave witness that when people love the Lord, they act like they love the Lord! At the age of four, she understood that when you have Jesus, you look differently, you act differently, and you speak differently. That reminder caused this mommy to soften and realize that the important thing for the morning was not to be on time for a Bible study but to model a life that reflected my love for the Author of the Book.

One thing I have learned through the years as a wife, mother of four, grandmother of eleven, and observer of many is that our love leaks. We start out at the altar saying, "I will love you for better or worse." Then the worse comes, and we get angry, allowing emotional walls to build up and separate us. We have friendships that are priceless, and then difficult situations arise and our connections slowly fade. The same can be true of our love relationship with God. We have seasons where we feel close to Him, and then suddenly we find ourselves feeling estranged and distant. This is what happened to the Israelites while they were in exile: they found themselves in a pagan nation, no longer exposed to the worship of their God, and their hearts grew cold toward Him. Nehemiah wanted to remind the people who God is and that His love is everlasting. He did this by bringing songs of praise back into the city.

Praising God is expressing our thanks and honor to Him. If we are going to give someone praise, we must remember who they are and what they have done for us. The Book of Psalms is a collection of beautiful poetry. The Hebrew title of the book translates to "Praises." The word *psalm* means "songs." There are over 150 songs recorded that were used in the Jewish worship services, accompanied by lyres, flutes, horns and cymbals. Each of these songs displays the character of God and the testimony of what He has accomplished for His people. Read Psalm 136:1–26.

The Israelites were continually forgetting God's character and all He did for them. Each line in Psalm 136 is a reminder of all His great deeds and revealed character. With each verse of the song, the people are reminded of who their God is: Creator, Deliverer, Savior, Protector, and Guide. The repetitiveness of the line "His faithful love endures forever" (Psalm 136:1 NIV) is the psalmist's way of reminding the people of God's faithful and eternal love, no matter how far they had strayed in their love relationship with Him. I imagine that this song did for the Israelites what my sweet daughter's song did for me, snapping them back to the reality that they were God's children and they needed to acknowledge Him by praising Him for all His great deeds. Not only was their spiritual condition dependent upon them being keepers of praise, but future generations' spiritual condition was dependent upon it as well.

Reflect and Respond

It has been thirty-three years since the day my daughter sang me her song. Recently, her sweet four-year-old daughter was playing at my home, singing the chorus of a popular contemporary Christian song by 7eventh Time Down, "God Is on the Move."

> I know—I know—God is on the move, on the move
> Hallelujah
> God is on the move in many mighty ways
> God is on the move, on the move Hallelujah
> God is on the move on the move today

What joy this brought to my heart as I rejoiced in realizing the praises of my daughter's heart did not stop as a child but continued and, now she has passed on those praises to my grandchildren. It is our calling to tell the stories of what our God has done—not only the stories of the Bible but what has He personally done for us. The generations that follow will never know if we don't tell them.

Fight

Is your love for God more distant than in times past?

Consider your attitude and actions today. Do they reflect an intimate relationship with God, or one that has grown distant and cold? It is important to know the answer because if your heart has grown cold toward God, you will be missing out on praising Him.

Build

To become a keeper of praise, we must remember what God has done for us. Take time to insert your own story of what God has done for you into the verses of Psalm 136 (HCSB). Here is my example to get you started.

Give thanks to the LORD for He is good.
His faithful love endures forever.
As a rebellious child He redeemed and rescued me
His faithful love endures forever.
When seeking Love, He graced me with a godly husband.
His faithful love endures forever.
During my deepest loss, He healed my broken heart.
His faithful love endures forever.

When you have finished writing your song, spend some time praising God for all the great deeds He has done for you. Share your song with someone.

Day Five

The Day I Almost Broke!

Today's scripture reading: Nehemiah 8:8–12

I almost broke in the spring of 1982. One month after we had buried our infant son from birth complications, our church was having a get-together. As the pastor and his wife, we felt we needed to attend, though the thought of festivities was the last thing on my mind. Our regular sitter wasn't available, but eventually I found a friend's daughter who was able to help. After about thirty minutes at the party, however, I received a phone call from the babysitter saying she needed me to come home for a minute. As we entered the home, the mother of the teenager informed us that while the sitter had been on the phone, the children had gone for a walk, and they had been unsuccessful in finding them. Three children, ages six, four, and two, were lost.

According to the census, there were 122 people, 45 households, and 32 families residing in our small community. However, most of the homes were rural. Literally there were only a few streets with homes within the city limits, and our home was one block from the state highway that ran through town. Like most little communities, if you blinked, you missed it. For hours our community searched, but as the evening sun went down, my concern turned to fear and eventually to panic. Feeling myself begin to lose control of my emotions, I walked back into my empty house and cried out to God. As my mind raced quickly to all the worst-case scenarios of what had become of my children, my weeping turned to sobs as I cried out, asking God why He had allowed someone to take all my children. In that moment, I knew what it meant to be broken. Everything within me was straining to hold on to my reason and sanity.

Then I heard the horns, the car pulling up, and people shouting. The children came running into my arms, crying and confused. Words of explanations of where they were spilled out, but nothing at that moment mattered. They were home, safe, alive, and mine! The search party went away, the children were put safely to bed, and I fell into the arms of my husband. I'll never forget the words he spoke to me. "Carol, this was not of God. This was of Satan, and we will not let him win!"

In Numbers 18, we learn that the Levites are the priests of God who, among other duties, offer sacrifices to God on behalf of the people. In Nehemiah 8:8, they are also the ones who explained God's law to the Israelites, an effort that brought truth to the forefront rather than worry, fear, and doubt. Just as the Levites spoke truth to the Israelites, so my husband spoke truth and comfort to my soul; in that moment, he was my Levite.

The enemy had almost broken me: he had whispered in my ear that my God was against me. My thoughts had gone to faithlessness, and my hope had been displaced, but in those few short words of truth, I was reminded that my God is a God of love and grace. Only Satan would have orchestrated such an evil plan to attempt to destroy us at a time when we were weak and vulnerable. We chose not to let that night define our future. We chose not to remain fearful, angry, and questioning. We chose to believe the truth of who our God is and to rejoice in God's provision of wholeness.

Nehemiah 1:3 (HCSB) says, "They said to me, "The remnant in the province, who survived the exile, are in great trouble and disgrace. Jerusalem's wall has been broken down, and its gates have been burned down."

Our city is not surrounded by a broken, crumbled wall, but our nation, cities, neighborhoods, friends, and families are broken and in disgrace. Christian homes are crumbling at a staggering rate. Even our youth, raised in Christian homes, are leaving their faith. Pastors are abandoning the ministry. Yes, our world is broken. It is only when we take the Word of

God and align our thinking, actions, and belief system to that truth that we find wholeness. As keepers of the faith, we are called to be Levites, stand up, and speak God's truth to restore the people to wholeness.

Reflect and Respond

The Word of God, the Bible, is as essential to our spiritual lives as food is to our physical lives. It should be read daily, and its truths should be obeyed. When we meditate on the scriptures, they bring profit to our lives by growing us spiritually and giving us meaning. The Bible gives us hope by pointing to the way we can become who God designed us to be. When we know the truth of the scriptures, our spiritual lives will grow, we will become fruitful in our service to the Lord, and we will prepare the way for others to come to know His truth.

Fight

The Bible is the only book in which we can put our trust for the truth. No other book is inspired of God, through the Holy Spirit, to reveal God's truth without any error. The Bible is our book of truth from our trustworthy God. If we are going to be spokespeople for God's truth, we must know, understand, and obey this book. In what ways did your actions today reveal that you trust the scriptures?

Build

Consider some creative ways you can come to know and understand the scriptures better, such as enrolling in a local college or online Bible course, attending a weekly Bible study small group, or purchasing a Bible study course and doing it with a small group in your home. Decide to actively begin studying the Bible.

Day Six

Burdens of Joy

While driving to my grandparents' home, I could feel my excitement of seeing them again; visits had been too few and far between as of late. I could hear Grandma calling to Grandpa that we had arrived even before I entered their home. Within moments, Grandpa came around the corner, and what was tagging along beside him stopped me short. It wasn't the fact that this matted, ungroomed creature had to be the ugliest dog I had ever laid eyes on. It wasn't his teeth that visibly protruded several inches out from his lower lip. I even think I could have overlooked his big brown eyes that appeared to be ready to pop out of their sockets at any moment. No, all these characteristics would have been almost expected from a dearly loved shih tzu loving owned by aging, common country folks. What caused my shock was the milk jug that was tied around his neck. Yes, I said milk jug. To be more specific, a one-gallon milk jug filled halfway with dirt, attached to a small rope, and tied around his neck. Every step little Fido took was accompanied by the plopping sound of the jug dragging along beside him. Now, before you pick up the phone and call the Humane Society, let me explain: dear little Fido was an escape artist. Every time he went out, he dug under the fence and ran off. Fearing for his safety, and because they were too elderly to chase after him, Grandpa came up with the perfect solution: tie a milk jug around his neck so he couldn't fit under the fence to escape. The amazing thing was this little happy pup seemed perfectly content with the burden of the solution to keep him safe and protected by those who loved him.

Read Nehemiah 8:1–12 (HCSB).

All the people gathered together at the square in front of the Water Gate. They asked Ezra the scribe to bring the book of the law of Moses that the LORD had given Israel. On the first day of the seventh month, Ezra the priest brought the law before the assembly of men, women, and all who could listen with understanding. While he was facing the square in front of the Water Gate, he read out of it from daybreak until noon before the men, the women, and those who could understand. All the people listened attentively to the book of the law. Ezra the scribe stood on a high wooden platform made for this purpose. Mattithiah, Shema, Anaiah, Uriah, Hilkiah, and Maaseiah stood beside him on his right; to his left were Pedaiah, Mishael, Malchijah, Hashum, Hash-baddanah, Zechariah, and Meshullam. Ezra opened the book in full view of all the people, since he was elevated above everyone. As he opened it, all the people stood up. Ezra praised the LORD, the great God, and with their hands uplifted all the people said, "Amen, Amen!" Then they bowed down and worshiped the LORD with their faces to the ground. Jeshua, Bani, Sherebiah, Jamin, Akkub, Shabbethai, Hodiah, Maaseiah, Kelita, Azariah, Jozabad, Hanan, and Pelaiah, who were Levites,] explained the law to the people as they stood in their places. They read out of the book of the law of God, translating and giving the meaning so that the people could understand what was read. Nehemiah the governor, Ezra the priest and scribe, and the Levites who were instructing the people said to all of them, "This day is holy to the LORD your God. Do not mourn or weep." For all the people were weeping as they heard the words of the law. Then he said to them, "Go and eat what is rich, drink what is sweet, and send portions to those who have nothing prepared, since today is holy to our Lord. Do not grieve, because the joy of the LORD is your stronghold." And the Levites quieted all the people, saying, "Be still, since today is holy. Do not grieve." Then all the people began to eat and drink, send portions, and have a great celebration, because they had understood the words that were explained to them.

Notice in this passage that the word *people* and the phrase "all the people" are mentioned numerous times. Nehemiah had successfully rebuilt the wall and dealt with the opposition, and now it was time to focus on the people by bringing them back to the truth of God's Word. The Jews had just spent seventy years in captivity in Babylon. During this time, they were restricted in their freedom to practice their religion, and they had limited access to the law of God. Whatever they knew of their faith came mostly from what others passed down to them, so after seventy years, they had likely forgotten most of what they knew of God's law. Therefore, Nehemiah assembled fifty thousand people to hear the reading of the Word. The Levites, as keepers of God's truth, were disbursed among the crowd so they could make clear the true meaning of the scriptures. When the people began understanding the truth of what they were hearing, they were deeply grieved and fell under conviction. The more they heard, the more they realized just how much they had disobeyed the will of God, and they wept over their sins.

When we realize we have offended God by our rebellion and disobedience, it should generate remorse in our hearts. We should grieve and be sorrowful because such sorrow brings us to repentance and leads us to salvation. Yet notice what Nehemiah said to the people in verse 10 (HCSB): "Do not grieve because the joy of the LORD is your stronghold." Another translation says, "the joy of the LORD is your strength" (NIV). Many times when we read the scriptures, we become so focused on the guilt of our sins that we remain in grief and despair and do not move toward obedience. Nehemiah warned the people to stop weeping and move on to joy.

God's laws are not meant to burden us. First John 5:3–4 (HCSB) says, "For this is what love for God is: to keep His commands. Now

His commands are not a burden, because whatever has been born of God conquers the world. This is the victory that has conquered the world: our faith." The truth of God's Word is our victory, and it is through the hearing and the obeying of scriptures that we obtain righteous living. The people could move beyond guilt and shame to repentance and joy because they understood the truth of scripture. The joy of the Lord comes from properly understanding the truth of God's Word.

Reflect and Respond

The milk jug around the neck of my grandparent's dog may have appeared restrictive, even perhaps abusive, but the intention was to keep the dog in the boundaries of safety. In the yard, the dog was protected, fed, and cared for. Outside the gate was danger, starvation, and the potential for death. God has given us His word to keep us safe within the arms of our Master. How exciting to know His word is His provision for bringing us to a personal relationship with Jesus, so that we can know Him and know His will for our lives. As keepers of the faith, we must be obedient to the keeping of God's truths.

Fight

Many times when we read the scriptures, we are like the Israelites and become burdened with the reality of our sins; guilt and shame overwhelm us. Remember, though, that Jesus came so we might have abundant life (see John 10:10). Turn your weeping into joy today by understanding the truth of the scriptures.

Build

Write down some instances where obeying the scriptures brought you freedom from guilt, shame, and potential danger.

What are some rewards you have found in keeping the scriptures?

Be joyful and celebrate God's mercy and grace today; read Psalm 19:7–11.

Day Seven

Living a Life Worth Remembering

Today's scripture reading: Nehemiah 5:19

Several years ago, I had the privilege of helping an elderly couple relocate from their country home of many years into a smaller home within city limits. Knowing his time in this world was soon to be over, the husband placed himself and his wife into a more suitable home for their retirement years. I don't think he realized just how soon his homecoming would be, and just two weeks after their closing date, I walked into his funeral, sadly realizing I knew very little about this man. Yet as a lovely video flashed on the screen, I saw a glimpse of who he was. Photos told the story of a life lived with his lovely wife of fifty-plus years, four children, and many beautiful grandchildren. Midway through the service, friends and family testified how their hearts were changed for the better by living side by side with this kind-hearted, gentle soul. After observing the details of this man's life, it was obvious that he not only lived a good life but also left a godly legacy. Right then and there, I redetermined in my heart that I would do the same. As I walked out of that funeral, my steps were lighter and my heart was full, knowing that someday I would have all of eternity to spend with my new friend.

It really matters how we live our lives.

Ladies, what if instead of waiting until our funeral to show others who we are, we live every moment of our lives as if someone who doesn't really know us is watching? Would our conversations reveal to them what our hearts are fighting for? Would the actions they observe reveal what our lives, lived out, are building? I wonder if, when they walk away from their time with us, whether that time is just a moment in passing or a lifetime shared, they will see women who are striving to live for something bigger than ourselves—not women desiring to just be good wives, good mothers, good friends, but women who determine in their hearts to add *godly* to their names.

You see, there is no higher compliment than to be called a godly woman, a woman who is striving to reflect the beauty of Jesus in all she does. Though by no means perfect, a godly woman is the woman who desires to love and serve the Lord more today than yesterday. She is a woman who, when we have spent time with her, creates within us a hunger for more of Jesus and inspires us to continue boldly in our faith and keep running the race. Isn't our desire as Christian women to not only live a good life but, most important, leave behind a legacy of faith?

The last chapter of Nehemiah closes in a prayer: "Remember me, my God, with favor" (Nehemiah 13: 14 NIV). Nehemiah was asking God to remember him not on the merits of his own good works but in God's loving-kindness. All through his life, Nehemiah called on the mercies of God. He started his journey on the basis that God was a gracious, loving Father who keeps His commands. Nehemiah based his ministry on the truth that if he remained faithful to do the will of the Lord, he would find God's favor because he served a promise-keeping God. He spent his life fulfilling God's vision by returning the people to the worship of the one true God. He had been faithful to bring them back to a place of praise and worship, and he saw to the return of scripture, bringing God's truth back to His people. At the end of his ministry, we see him asking God to remember him in His grace. He never imagined that he earned something from God; he was simply asking for God's unmerited favor to be upon him. He remained completely dependent upon the grace of God.

Reflect and Respond

We must realize that we are justified by grace alone, not our works. We want God to remember what we have accomplished for Him in our lives according to His grace and eternal love.

Fight

Who comes to mind when you think of godly women and how have they influenced your walk with the Lord?

When you consider your actions this past week, do you think others would conclude you are building a life for the glory of the Lord? Why or why not?

Build

Sometimes we feel too inadequate to be considered godly. Change your self-talk by putting to memory at least one of the following verses.

- Ephesians 2:10
- 1 John 3:1
- John 1:12–13

Epilogue

May we be encouraged and fully empowered, dear friend, knowing this journey God has commissioned us to is not one we take alone but rather in community together, arm in arm. May our steps be lighter and our hearts be fuller knowing, through the empowerment of the Holy Spirit, we can overcome every opposition coming against us.

It is our fervent prayer that you will stand firm to keep the faith and intentionally live a life worth remembering, leaving behind a godly legacy as you fight for what's right and build what last for the glory of our great God.

Thank you for spending time with us through the pages of this journal, mighty warrior!

Be empowered. "Don't be afraid of them. Remember the Lord, who is great and awesome, and fight for your families, your sons and your daughters, your wives and your homes" (Nehemiah 4:14 NIV).

WORTHY PURSUIT

ministries